Collins

Student Support Materials for
Edexcel A2 History

Unit 4

Historical enquiry

Written off

Series editor: Angela Leonard

Author: Rosemary Rees

William Collins' dream of knowledge for all began with the publication of his first book in 1819. A self-educated mill worker, he not only enriched millions of lives, but also founded a flourishing publishing house. Today, staying true to this spirit, Collins books are packed with inspiration, innovation and practical expertise. They place you at the centre of a world of possibility and give you exactly what you need to explore it.

Collins. Freedom to teach
Published by Collins
An imprint of HarperCollins*Publishers*
77 – 85 Fulham Palace Road
Hammersmith
London
W6 8JB

Browse the complete Collins catalogue at
www.collinseducation.com

10 9 8 7 6 5 4 3 2 1

ISBN-13 978 0 00 745745 8

Rosemary Rees asserts her moral rights to be identified as the author of this work

British Library Cataloguing in Publication Data
A Catalogue record for this publication is available from the British Library

Commissioned by Andrew Campbell
Project managed by Alexandra Riley and Shirley Wakley
Production by Simon Moore

Designed by Jouve
Edited by Dave Waddell and Joan Miller
Proofread by Sue Ecob, Rosalind Horton and Grace Glendinning
Indexed by Michael Forder
Illustrations by Ann Paganuzzi
Picture and text research by Grace Glendinning and Caroline Green
Cover picture research by Caroline Green
Cover design by Angela English

With special thanks to: Kimberley Atkins for devising the concept

Printed and bound by Printing Express Limited, Hong Kong

COVER: '14th-century vellum (calfskin) illuminated manuscript depicting knights in battle', The Art Gallery Collection/Alamy

Acknowledgements

The publishers gratefully acknowledge the permission granted to reproduce the copyright material in this book. While every effort has been made to trace and contact copyright holders, where this has not been possible the publishers will be pleased to make the necessary arrangements at the first opportunity.

p 38 from Lawrence James, *Raj: The Making and Unmaking of British India*, published 1997 by Little, Brown Book Group; p 41 from *The Tudor Years*, edited by John Lotherington and published by Hodder & Stoughton Educational Division Publication in 1994 © Hodder Education. Reproduced by permission of Hodder Education; p 53, 93, 94, 96 From NORTON. *A People and a Nation*, 8E. © 2008 Wadsworth, a part of Cengage Learning, Inc. Reproduced by permission. www.cengage.com/permissions; p 53, 93 & 96 From BOYER/CLARK/KETT/SALISBURY AT EL. *The Enduring Vision*, 6E. © 2008 Wadsworth, a part of Cengage Learning, Inc. Reproduced by permission. www.cengage.com/permissions; p 53 from Maldwyn Jones, *The limits of liberty: American history, 1607-1992*, published 1995. By permission of Oxford University Press; p 54 from Jonathan Phillips, *The Crusades 1095-1197*, published 2002 by Pearson Education; p 55 from Kerry Brown , 'Friends and Enemies: the Past, Present and Future of the Communist Party of China', 2009, Anthem Press. By permission of Wimbledon Publishing Company; p 56 from Barker, Juliet, *Conquest: The English Kingdom of France 1417-1450*, published in 2009 by Little, Brown Book Group; p 57 from G. R. Elton, *England under the Tudors*, published in 1955 by Methuen; p 58 from Gorgon Corrigan, *Blood, Sweat and Arrogance and the Myths of Churchill's War*, published in 2006 by Weidenfeld & Nicolson, © Orion Publishing Co.; p 59c from E. P. Thompson, *The Making of the English Working Class*, 1963, published by Pantheon and reprinted with permission from Penguin; p 59b from M. Hartwell, 'The Standard of Living', published in the *Economic History Review* in 1963 by John Wiley and Sons; p 62 from Barry Coward, *Oliver Cromwell*, published in 1991 by Longman/Pearson Education; p 63 from Richard Evans, *The Third Reich in Power*, published in 2005 by Allen Lane and reprinted with permission from Penguin; p 77t from Eric J Evans, *The Forging of the Modern State 1783-1870*, published in 2001 by Longman; p 77b from Martin Pugh, *The March of the Woman*, published in 2000. By permission of Oxford University Press; p 81 from a video of William Waheed discussing the Browder vs Gayle case. Quoted with permission from William Waheed ©Cosmo-D Productions, L.L.C., William Waheed; p 87 from the *Seattle Post Intelligencer*, 9 December 1941. Reprinted with permission from Hearst Communications, Inc.; p 94t from Hugh Brogan, *The Penguin History of the United States of America*, 1990. Reprinted by permission of Pearson Education, Inc., Upper Saddle River, New Jersey; p 94c from Gary Noy, *Distant Horizon: Documents from the nineteenth-century American West*, published in 1999 by University of Nebraska Press; p 95 & 96 from Maldwyn Jones *The limits of liberty: American history, 1607-1992*, published 1995. By permission of Oxford University Press; p 99 & 100t from *The Early Bourbon Monarchy in France, 1589–1661*, an internet resource produced by the University of Leicester; p 100c, 100b, 101t & 103c from Alan James, *The Origins of French Absolutism 1598–1661*, Pearson Longman, 2006; p 103b & 104t from *Europe: A History* by Norman Davies, published by Pimlico 2007. Reprinted by permission of The Random House Group Limited; p 107t, 108c, 110 from Kate Adie's broadcast, 'Kate Adie returns to Tiananmen Square', 3 June 2009. Quoted with permission from the BBC; p 107b, 108b, 109b, 110b from Jonathan Fenby, *The Penguin History of Modern China*, published in 2009 by Penguin; p 108t, 110b, 114c & 116b from SEARCH FOR MODERN CHINA, SECOND EDITION by Jonathan D. Spence. Copyright © 1999, 1990 by Jonathan D. Spence. Used by permission of W. W. Norton & Company, Inc.; p 108b, 109c, 110c, 115t from John Gittings, *The Changing Face of China from Mao to Market*, 2006. By permission of Oxford University Press; p 109c, 110t from Jasper Becker and John Gittings, *China at war with its people 'Thousands dead' as ruthless assault goes on - Wounded die for lack of care*. Guardian News & Media Ltd 5 June 1989; p 116 from *The Rise and Fall of Communism* by Archie Brown, published by Bodley Head 2009. Reprinted by permission of The Random House Group Limited; p 117t from J.A.G. Roberts, *A History of China*, 2006, Palgrave Macmillan. Reproduced with permission of Palgrave Macmillan.

The publisher would like to thank the following for permission to reproduce pictures in these pages (t = top, b = bottom, c = centre, l = left, r = right):

COVER : The Art Gallery Collection/Alamy, p 15 Popular Science Monthly Volume 3/WikiMedia Commons, p 25a sphtc.org/WikiMedia Commons, p 25b WikiMedia Commons, p 25c, 25g & 44 Library of Congress/WikiMedia Commons, p 25d & 49 WikiMedia Commons, p 25e Granger Collection/WikiMedia Commons, p 25f Hung Chung Chih/Shutterstock, p 25h Royal Collection, London/WikiMedia Commons, p 29 Shaw, Fred Kirk/WikiMedia Commons, p 34t © Andrew Dunn/WikiMedia Commons, p 34b Gaetano Images Inc./Alamy, p 48 1956 Herblock Cartoon, copyright by The Herb Block Foundation, p 51 Badge of the Five Wounds of Christ (embroidered textile), English School, (16th century) / His Grace The Duke of Norfolk, Arundel Castle / The Bridgeman Art Library, p 50 The Art Gallery Collection/Alamy.

Contents

Essential notes

The coursework programme is the historical theme, covering at least 100 years, within which you will carry out your investigation. You will be taught an overview of the coursework programme and the main themes before you make up your mind about your enquiry. The programme you are following and within which you set up your enquiry may be one of Edexcel's programmes ranging from 'Roman Britain c.43–c.300' to 'Twentieth Century International Relations 1879–1980', or a different programme that has been approved by Edexcel.

Moderators' notes

A contemporary source is a source that was created during the timeframe of your coursework programme. Some students make the mistake of evaluating secondary sources. Make sure your source is contemporary.

What is this unit about?

The key to understanding this unit lies in the title 'Historical enquiry'. You will research your own enquiry, find your own source material and link this with what you know to reach a well-thought out, balanced judgement. You can spend time over doing this, too, and so in many ways you are working as a historian would do.

How is the unit structured?

You have to write one assignment that is divided into two parts. Each part has a separate focus.

In **Part A** (a **depth enquiry**) you will need to research the short-term significance of an event or a factor such as an individual, development or movement. You will need to ask, 'What difference did this make?'

In **Part B** (a **breadth enquiry**) you will need to research the process of change over the whole timeframe of your coursework programme. You will need to set your chosen event or factor in a broader context, investigating the process of change within the wider timeframe.

What skills will you need to show?

You will need to show different skills in Part A and Part B.

In Part A you need to show that you can:

- assess the significance of your chosen factor or event in the short term
- interpret, evaluate and use contemporary sources in their historical context.

In Part B you need to show that you can:

- sort out issues that are relevant to your enquiry, by reading widely
- assess the significance of your chosen event or factor in the long term (at least 100 years) by linking it with other events and forces for change.

How will your work be marked?

You will not have your work marked 'right' or 'wrong'. Instead, your work will be marked according to the level of skill and understanding you have shown.

Two Assessment Objectives will be used. Part A of your assignment will be marked using Assessment Objectives 1 and 2a. Part B of your assignment will be marked using Assessment Objective 1.

Objective 1 assesses:

- your ability to select and deploy historical knowledge and to communicate your understanding of history
- your ability to analyse and explain key concepts such as causation, consequence, change and significance.

Objective 2a assesses:

- your ability to analyse and evaluate a range of source material.

Just how this works is shown in the ladder diagrams below. Of course you will want to get as high up the ladder as possible, in order to gain maximum marks. This book will show you how to do this.

Assessment Objective 1

Level 5: A completely analytical response directly exploring the process of change. (Level 5 is only in Part B)

Level 4: An analytical response well focused on the enquiry.

Level 3: A broadly analytical response but with some descriptive passages.

Level 2: Developed, relevant statements that are linked together.

Level 1: A series of simple statements, only partly relevant to the enquiry.

Assessment Objective 2a

Level 4: A wide range of sources selected to investigate the enquiry, thoroughly questioned and the evidence from this used to make and support judgements where the status of the evidence is considered.

Level 3: A range of sources selected to develop the enquiry, interpreted and put in their right historical context. Weight given to evidence when making judgements that are based on cross-referencing and using the sources as a set.

Level 2: A range of relevant source material identified, put in their right historical context and interpreted beyond their surface features. Weight given to evidence when making judgements.

Level 1: Some relevant source material identified, understood and put in their right historical context; some simple evaluation and judgements made.

Moderators' notes

There are two important things to note at this stage:

- Your research should be independent.

- You must write grammatically and express yourself clearly.

Moderators' notes

An analytical response is one that doesn't just 'tell the story'. Rather, it seeks to explain what was happening and, in doing so, bring out the key elements of the enquiry.

Moderators' notes

Supported judgements are judgements where evidence is provided to show how the judgement was reached.

Moderators' notes

In using evidence to reach a judgement, it will be necessary to decide how much importance is to be placed on each piece of evidence. This is what is meant by 'considering the status of the evidence'.

Moderators' notes

Cross-referencing occurs when one source is compared with another. This could be in terms of, for example, content, date, or authorship. Cross-referencing can be for agreement or challenge.

Essential notes

The full mark schemes can be found on pages 122–23.

Getting the title right

Successful historical enquiries begin with asking the right kind of questions. In this respect, the quality of the title of an assignment is vital. A well-constructed title:

- helps shape your answer
- gives an indication as to where to begin and finish an enquiry
- signposts the direction in which to go
- focuses on areas of importance
- shows the moderator that you know what you are doing.

Depth study

Part A is what is called a depth study. This means that you will be looking in-depth at how an event, individual or factor makes a significant contribution to the history contained within the coursework programme you are following.

There are two golden rules when working out an enquiry title for Part A. It must focus on short-term significance and it must look at outcomes.

Part A enquiry should provide the answer to the following key questions:

- What impact did the event/individual/factor have?
- What did the event/individual/factor bring about?
- What difference did the event/individual/factor make?

Constructing Part A titles

When constructing titles for the first time, it is easy to make mistakes. Look at the five titles below. Only one of them works as a Part A title.

1. 'To what extent was giving the vote to some women in 1918 the result of the activities of the suffragettes?'

2. 'How significant was W. E. Gladstone in bringing about change in the relationship between Ireland and the United Kingdom in the years 1815–1922?'

3. 'To what extent can we blame Richard III for the murder of the Princes in the Tower?'

4. 'Was Yasser Arafat a force for good in the Middle East in the years 1996–2004?'

5. 'What, in your view, was the short-term impact of the emancipation of the peasants (1857–61) on Russian government and society?'

Moderators' notes

'Short term' is a period of time that is not more than 20% of the time span of the coursework programme being followed. That is 20 years for every 100 years studied. However, this is the maximum. It can be as short as 12 months. The actual time span will depend on the significance of the individual, event or factor being studied, and where you decided to focus the depth of your enquiry. For example, a title investigating: 'The impact of the Versailles Treaty on international relations' would need to limit the enquiry to 'between 1919 and 1929' in order for it to be considered short term.

Title 5 is a proper Part A title. The other four titles are not. The Moderators' notes on the right tell you why.

Improving a weak title

Look again at the titles on page 6. It is relatively easy to turn the first four titles round so that they focus on outcomes and on short-term significance:

1. 'What was the short-term impact of the activities of the suffragettes?'
2. 'What was the short-term impact of W. E. Gladstone on the relationship between Britain and Ireland?'
3. 'What was the short-term significance of the supposed murder of the Princes for Richard III and the monarchy?'
4. 'Assess the short-term significance of Yasser Arafat for political relationships within the Middle East.'

Focusing on outcomes

An outcome is the result of an action or an event. Usually a significant action/event will result in a number of outcomes, some more significant than others. Your enquiry should focus on discovering and investigating a range of outcomes.

All four of the above amended titles now successfully focus on outcomes, and will therefore enable the students following them to look for a range of different outcomes.

The first enquiry may lead the student to research the impact of suffragette activities on parliament, the government, the police, public opinion and the suffragists.

The second enquiry may lead the student to research the impact of Gladstone on British–Irish relationships; as in the reaction of Irish and English politicians and politics, the Irish and English press and Irish and English public opinion.

The third enquiry may lead the student to research the reactions of Richard III, Henry Tudor, various nobles (especially Buckingham), foreign observers and English commentators to the disappearance and alleged murder of the Princes.

The fourth enquiry may lead the student to research the reactions of the USA, Israel and the United Nations, Hamas, Fatah and the world press to the various actions and activities of Yasser Arafat.

Moderators' notes

The suffragette enquiry does not focus on the difference made by suffragette activities.

The Gladstone enquiry covers far too long a time span. It is also firmly focused on change, which is more appropriate for a Part B enquiry.

The Princes enquiry is really asking who murdered the two princes. It is not focused on the outcome of the death of the princes, and on the difference this made.

The Yasser Arafat enquiry looks at the significance of an individual within a short timeframe. However, by using the word 'good', it becomes subjective, as 'good' means different things to different people.

The emancipation enquiry is an excellent title, it clearly focuses on impact in the short term.

Essential notes

It is very important that your enquiry title is grammatically correct. When speaking of significance, always ask 'what is the significance *of … for …*'.

However, when speaking of impact, always ask 'what is the impact *of … on …*'.

Choosing the Part A focus

Part A of your assignment will be an in-depth investigation into the short-term significance of an event, individual or factor.

In making an informed choice with regard to what you decide to investigate, make sure you:

* organise your ideas whilst learning about a particular subject
* think carefully about the 'question stem' in your enquiry title
* note the short-term significance of an event, individual or factor
* have enough contemporary source material with which to work.

Organising your ideas

As you work through the introductory course with your teacher, you should be thinking about the areas within which you would like to focus your enquiry. These will be significant events, individuals and factors that were involved in the process of change. You will find it helpful to organise your initial thinking by jotting down your ideas into a grid like the one below, which you can copy into your coursework file. Here is one that has been started by a student following the Edexcel-designed coursework Unit CW39: *The USA: from Reconstruction to Civil Rights c1877–1981*:

Events	Individuals	Factors
The Jim Crow laws 1887–91	Marcus Garvey	Growth of the Union Pacific Railroad 1862–81
The Quota Act 1921	Rosa Parks	Growth of the car industry 1913–29
		The New Deal 1933–39

Choosing the question 'stem'

Your enquiry is going to be an in-depth investigation. Because it is an investigation, you do not want simply to describe what you have found out. You are going to have to show how you have evaluated evidence using contemporary sources, and how you have used this evidence to reach a judgement. At the same time, you will also need to demonstrate an in-depth knowledge of the period you are investigating. To do all this, it is important to start your enquiry using one of the following question stems:

* What was the short-term significance of … ?
* What was the short-term impact of … ?
* Assess the impact of …
* How significant was … ?
* Assess the significance of …
* How important were the consequences of … ?

Trying out enquiry titles

At this point, you will have completed the grid of events, factors and individuals that you think might be suitable for an in-depth enquiry. Now use that grid, together with the question stems, to work out some enquiry titles.

The next grid is an example of one that has been started by a student following the Edexcel-designed coursework Unit CW39: *The USA: from Reconstruction to Civil Rights c1877–1981*. You could follow this example, using the individuals, events and factors you have already listed that relate to your own coursework programme.

Focus of enquiry	Significance	Enquiry title
Rosa Parks	Public demonstration of opposition to segregation on public transport Led to Montgomery Bus Boycott Helped to launch Martin Luther King to national prominence in civil rights movement	Assess the short-term significance of Rosa Parks in the years 1955–57.
The Jim Crow laws	Segregation in schools, public places and public transport Black/white inter-marriage forbidden in some states Segregation in US military Unsuccessfully challenged (1896) in Louisiana by Homer Plessy	What, in your view, was the short-term significance of the Jim Crow laws in the years 1887–96?
The New Deal	Shift in political and domestic policy Increased federal control of economy Beginning of social programmes Growth in power of trades unions	Assess the impact of the New Deal on the USA in the years 1933–39.

Checking whether your enquiry works

By now, you will have selected the topic that is going to form the basis of your Part A enquiry and written the question that will become the title of your enquiry.

However, there are three important questions you must answer before beginning your enquiry, without which you will not be able to start:

1. Have you a good range of relevant contemporary sources with which to support your enquiry?

2. Have you a satisfactory range of secondary sources with which to put the enquiry in its correct historical context?

3. Have you thought of a range of important issues worth exploring as part of the enquiry?

The table below helps answer these questions. Copy it and list the necessary information. Do not forget to make a note of where you found your sources – you will need to find them again, and acknowledge them in your assignment. Remember: research your lists carefully.

Can I find ...	1	2	3	4	5
Five relevant and different contemporary sources?					
Three to five secondary sources that will help me put my enquiry in its correct historical context?					
Four to five different issues worth exploring?					

Points to consider when making your choice of individual

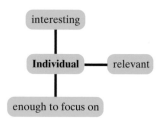

Enquiries focusing on individuals

If you decide to focus your Part A enquiry on a historical figure, it is important that you choose your subject carefully. The diagram on the left outlines the main points to consider when making your choice.

Choosing someone relevant

The individual you choose must be relevant to your coursework programme and must generate enough material for you to work on. It also helps if you find the person interesting!

Student 1

This student is following the Edexcel-designed coursework programme CW8: *The Changing Role of Parliament in England, 1529–1629.*

- The focus of this unit is the changing nature and role of parliaments, and the extent to which parliamentary power and its role within government changed throughout the period.

- The student is particularly interested in the statesman Francis Walsingham, and is considering investigating his short-term significance for Part A of the coursework assignment.

Will the choice work?

Walsingham was clearly working for Elizabeth I during the timeframe of the coursework programme, and was certainly heavily involved in the politics of the period. But what exactly did he have to do with the changing nature and role of parliaments? This student would struggle to make Walsingham's work as a spy-master relevant.

The student would be much better advised to choose someone closely involved with the workings of parliament, for example Thomas Cromwell or the Duke of Buckingham, George Villiers.

Student 2

This student is following the Edexcel-designed coursework programme CW37: *The Changing Nature of Warfare c1845–1991.*

- The focus of this unit is the influence of new technology on warfare; that is the ways in which, and the reasons why, the nature of warfare changed during the years 1845–1991.

- The timeframe easily covers Britain's participation in the Crimean War (1853–56). The student is particularly interested in the work done by Florence Nightingale at Scutari and whether or not she made a difference to the survival rates of the soldiers.

Will the choice work?

Florence Nightingale was clearly involved in the Crimean War and with the welfare of the troops, but look again at the coursework focus. She had nothing to do with the influence of new technology on warfare. This student would struggle to link Nightingale's work to the changing nature of warfare. The student would be better advised to choose someone such as Robert E. Lee or Air Chief Marshal Sir Arthur Harris.

Clearly, as Students 1 and 2 discovered, the person you choose as the focus of your Part A enquiry must be connected in a direct way with the focus of your coursework programme. Don't make it difficult for yourself. Choose someone who is directly relevant to the coursework focus.

Choosing what to focus on in an important individual

The list of individuals you have made will include some of the people who were of great importance. They will be really significant in the short term in having an impact on – and making a difference to – the time in which they lived. Of course you may choose one of them, but you do need to be careful. Consider the following student example:

Student 3

This student is following the Edexcel-designed coursework programme CW45: *Dictatorship and Revolution in Russia and the Soviet Union 1825–2000.*

- The focus of this coursework programme is on the nature and extent of change in the nature of government, society and economy in Russia and the Soviet Union over the period and the relationship between government and the governed over the period.

- The student has devised this Part A enquiry: 'What, in your view, was the short-term significance of Vladimir Ilyich Lenin?'

Will the choice work?

The question stem is correct, and Lenin is clearly relevant to the coursework programme. But there are two interconnected problems:

- Lenin was such an important figure in Russian history that the student would have problems in finding a sharp enough focus for a depth study within the assignment's word limit, which is 2000 words.

- Because Lenin was so important, there will be hundreds of contemporary sources to choose from. The student would have problems working through all the contemporary sources and selecting the ones to use.

To focus the enquiry, Student 3 decided to limit it to: 'What, in your view, was the short-term significance of Vladimir Ilyich Lenin during the Russian Civil War 1917–23?'

Notice that the student has limited the enquiry to a single main event, and has timeframed the enquiry through the inclusion of dates. The change in focus allows the student to carry out an in-depth investigation of an important individual without losing their way.

Essential notes

Lenin led the October Revolution of 1917 and the Russian Civil War (1917–23). He was the informal leader of the Russian Communist Party, 1903–24, and Chairman of the Council of People's Commissars of the Soviet Union, 1922–4. His revolutionary, Marxist writings were hugely influential amongst those wanting to overthrow their rulers.

Moderators' notes

Make sure your choice of individual is **interest-led**, that the individual is **relevant** to the coursework focus, and that the **scope of enquiry is limited** in order that it is sharply focused.

Points to consider when making your choice of event

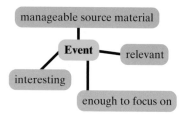

Essential notes

The French Revolution (1789–99) overthrew the monarchy and set up a republic that became increasingly violent. Inspired by the French Revolution, groups of people in Britain formed so-called 'corresponding societies'. These societies corresponded with each other, sharing ideas about the way Britain should be governed. The government, afraid of revolution, banned the corresponding societies in 1799.

Moderators' notes

The list of events you have made will include some whose significance is such that their impact can be traced across large time spans, and through a multitude of areas. These events have long- and short-term outcomes. Should you decide to choose such an event it is vital that you limit the scope of your enquiry. Remember to make your Part A enquiry into the short-term significance of an event both **relevant** and **manageable**.

Enquiries focusing on events

If you decide to focus your Part A enquiry on an event, it is important that you choose it carefully. The diagram on the left outlines the main points to consider when making your choice.

Choosing a relevant event

Remember that all coursework programmes have a clearly defined focus, and the event must be relevant to the coursework programme you are following. Consider the three student examples below, which all focus in different ways on the relevancy of certain kinds of events.

Student 4

This student is following the Edexcel-designed coursework programme CW14: *Challenging Authority: from Corresponding Societies to Trade Unions 1789–1889*.

- The programme's main focus is the changing relationship between British protestors and the British authorities, and the impact of protest on the period in question.

- The student is particularly interested in the French Revolution, and is considering investigating its short-term significance for Part A of the coursework assignments.

Will the choice work?

There is a link between the French Revolution and the British corresponding societies: they were inspired by the same idea. This is what the student wants to address. But the focus of the programme is protest in Britain, not France. This student would struggle to look at the short-term significance of the French Revolution in this context.

The student would be much better advised to focus on the British corresponding societies, and in particular on the London Corresponding Society. This way the student could limit the investigation to the society's short-term significance. This would mean concentrating on the formation of the society, the reaction of the British authorities, and the impact of its formation. The student would only be expected to mention the French Revolution in so much as its ideas influenced the society, and in terms of the British authorities making links between the society and France.

Student 5

This student is following the Edexcel-designed coursework programme CW40: *Twentieth Century International Relations 1879–1980*.

- The focus of the coursework programme is on the changing relationships between the powers and the ways in which this affected the balance of power throughout the period.

- The student has devised the following Part A enquiry: 'What, in your view, was the short-term significance of the signing of the Treaty of Versailles (1919)?'

Will the choice work?

This would seem, at first sight, to be an appropriate event for an enquiry. Its focus corresponds with the focus of the coursework programme. It has an appropriate question stem. However, the length of time involved in investigating Versailles's short-term significance raises three problems:

1. This student might decide to look at a period of about 20 years – from 1919–39. This would take the enquiry through a very complex period of international history, in which case the student would find it difficult to keep within word limit guidelines.

2. The number of significant outcomes resulting from Versailles means the student's enquiry would lack the necessary depth. Also the sheer volume of contemporary sources would be unmanageable.

3. Whilst the Versailles Treaty was an international treaty agreed to by the Allies, it was a treaty that directly affected Germany. The student might be tempted to investigate the impact on Germany rather than on international relations.

In view of these problems, the student decided to limit the enquiry to: 'What, in your view, was the short-term impact of the signing of the Treaty of Versailles (1919) on international relations in the years to 1929?'

Events of local importance

Some events on your list may be of local importance. These are often very interesting and can involve original research, using source material that has not been used before.

Student 6

This student is following the Edexcel-designed coursework programme CW13: *The Impact of Industrialisation in Britain c1780–1914*.

- The focus of the programme is the significance of the Industrial Revolution and the process of industrialisation in changing the lives of the people in Britain and affecting the structure both of the economy and the workforce.

- For the Part A enquiry, the student has decided on the following investigation: 'What, in your view, was the short-term significance of the opening in 1784 of Quarry Bank Mill, Styal, Cheshire?'

Will the choice work?

The student will investigate the short-term significance of Quarry Bank from 1784 to 1810 – the maximum time frame allowed. This will cover the initial years of expansion and the provision of accommodation for apprentices and workers. It is a good decision regarding the significance of Quarry Bank Mill for the local community: the short-term significance of such a local event is easier to trace through relatively long time spans. Crucially, identifying these issues will allow the student to make relevant links with the coursework programme's national scope.

Essential notes

The Treaty of Versailles, 1919, was one of the peace treaties at the end of the First World War. Britain, France and the USA (the Allies) had different aims and objectives, and this was essentially a compromise agreement among them. Germany was not involved in the negotiations, but was simply told what had to be done, and had to accept responsibility for causing the war.

Essential notes

Quarry Bank Mill in Styal, Cheshire, was built in 1784 by the Manchester textile merchant, Samuel Greg. It was one of the first water-powered cotton mills, converting to steam power around 1810. More than half of the workers were children from workhouses, who were housed in a separate Apprentice House.

Enquiries focusing on factors

Making factors work

You will have made a list of factors – relating to your coursework programme – which influenced change at that time. If you are going to work with a factor, you will need, most importantly, to be interested in finding out how that factor worked in the short term. Then you will need to check it out for relevance and manageability. The examples below of what other students have done will help you to focus your own thoughts.

Student 7

This student is following the Edexcel-designed coursework programme CW2: *Continuity and change in Anglo-Saxon England c300–790.*

- The focus of the programme is the challenge to Roman control, and the formation and governance of Anglo-Saxon England.

- The student has worked out the following Part A enquiry: 'What, in your view, was the short-term impact on Britain of the invasions of the Angles and Saxons?'

Will the choice work?

This enquiry should work well. This student has used an appropriate stem question. The student has chosen a workable factor – the invasion of Britain by the Angles and Saxons is well-documented, relatively easy to manage and raises important issues. The student has decided to use the maximum timeframe allowed – 100 years, a time frame that suits perfectly the impact of the factor.

Student 8

This student is following the Edexcel-designed coursework CW18: *The State and the Poor c1815–1939.*

- The focus of the programme is the changing attitudes to the poor throughout the period and the impact this had upon the ways in which state provision for the poor changed.

Essential notes

The invasion of Britain by the Angles and Saxons began in about CE367 and Saxon control was completed by about CE600.

Essential notes

John Stuart Mill (1806–73) was an English philosopher who developed the doctrine of utilitarianism. This doctrine maintained that an action was only right if it led to the greatest good for the greatest number of people. Utilitarianism heavily influenced the content of the 1834 Poor Law Amendment Act (which established a workhouse system), and impacted on the thinking of the Poor Law commissioners, who drew up rules and regulations that ensured the Act was appropriately implemented.

- The student wants to investigate the theory of utilitarianism that underpinned early 19th-century attitudes to poverty. The title of the Part A enquiry is: 'What, in your view, was the short-term significance of the doctrine of utilitarianism for the treatment of poverty in Britain in the years 1834–45?'

Will the choice work?

Again, this is a well-thought out enquiry title: it contains an appropriate stem question, a recognised and important philosophical doctrine (the factor) and a tight timeframe. The student will have no trouble finding evidence with which to support the ideas, and the issues fit very well with the programme's focus.

Student 9

This student is following the Edexcel-designed coursework programme *CW21: Britain and India 1845–1947*.

- The focus of the programme is on changing attitudes to empire in Britain and India, and on the changing ways in which Britain controlled and dismantled its empire in India.

- The student has worked out the following Part A enquiry: 'What, in your view, was the short-term significance of Indian rebellions against the British?'

Will the choice work?

No, it won't! The factor 'Indian rebellions' is far too vague. The moderator will ask: which rebellions and when? The student would be better advised to focus the enquiry on the short-term significance of one rebellion. The Indian Mutiny of 1857 would be a good one as there are plenty of contemporary sources related to the Mutiny and the student will be able to really focus on short-term significance.

John Stuart Mill, who developed the doctrine of utilitarianism

Moderators' notes

Edexcel defines 'short term' as being no more than 20% of the time span of the coursework programme. Remember this is a maximum: enquiries may focus on much shorter time spans if you think this is appropriate.

Essential note

The Indian Mutiny began as a mutiny of Indian soldiers of the British East India Company in Meerut in May 1857. It quickly spread across northern India. British forces eventually ended the rebellion in 1858.

Enquiries focusing on change

Your Part B enquiry must focus on the process of change across the whole time span of your coursework programme. This process of change is explored through an understanding of strands, factors and turning points.

Using strands to understand change

Your teacher will make sure that you have a clear overview of the coursework programme you are following. This involves introducing you to the main themes that run through the programme. These strands will differ depending on the coursework programme you are following. The importance of the strands is that they help you to understand what is really going on within the 'story' of the programme you are following. They will help you to think analytically. Here are two examples:

Moderators' notes

A 'strand' runs through the whole enquiry and identifies patterns of change. When identifying themes, it is important to remember that not all the themes play a significant part throughout the whole period. In the example in the first table, pressure from outside parliament played a considerable part in persuading parliament to pass the 1832 Reform Act, but much less in passing the 1867 Reform Act.

Example 1: Edexcel CW19 Representation and Democracy in Britain c1830–1931

Strands	Using strands to understand change
Reform	How much real change was there in the period?
Conservatism	To what extent was the existing system retained?
Revolution	To what extent was reform driven by fear of revolution?
Education	What was the impact of extending education to the working classes?
Popular pressure	How far was reform driven by pressure from outside parliament?
Democracy	What was meant by 'democracy' at this time, and how far was it achieved?
War	What impact did war (Crimean, Boer and First World War) have on bringing about change?

Example 2: Edexcel CW21 Britain and India 1845–1947

Strands	Using strands to understand change
Independence	What were the key events on the road to independence and partition?
The Raj	To what extent was the Raj an obstacle to change?
Indian nationalism	What was the impact of the growth of Indian nationalism in bringing about change?
Satyagraha	What part was played by civil disobedience campaigns?
Prominent individuals	What was the role of individuals in bringing about change?
War	To what extent did the First and Second World Wars change relationships between India and Britain?
Economy	What part did the economies of Britain and India play in changing the relationship between the two countries?

Using factors and turning points to investigate change

As you work through the introductory course, you should be thinking about factors that brought about change, and about specific events that marked the process of change – known as turning points. One of these – a factor or a turning point – will form the focus of your Part B enquiry.

It doesn't matter which you choose, but you must be very clear that you will need to structure a turning point enquiry differently from a factor enquiry. These differences in approach will determine the way you undertake your research, and the way in which you write up your findings. Remember, too, that you must research change over the whole period of the coursework programme.

Working with factors

If you decide to work with a title that focuses on factors that brought about change, you will need to select a factor that you believe was significant. The following enquiries are examples of working with factors:

- 'Assess the significance of Indian nationalism (1845–1947) in changing Britain's relationship with its empire in India.'
- 'Assess the significance of popular pressure in bringing about greater democracy in Britain 1830–1931.'
- 'Assess the significance of the role of individuals for the growth of Spanish power in the years 1474–1598.'

As you research the factor you have chosen, remember the following important points:

- Your research will be into causation. This means that you are going to have to research why this factor led to change.
- You will have to assess the significance of your chosen factor by comparing it to alternative factors that were involved in the process of change.

Working with turning points

You will need to select a specific event you believe was a key turning point in the process of change over the whole period of the coursework programme. The following enquiries are examples of working with turning points:

- 'In considering the process of change in Russia 1682–1796, how far can the Poll Tax of 1724 be seen as a key turning point?'
- 'To what extent can the Emancipation Proclamation of 1863 be seen as a turning point in the making of the US as a nation in the years 1815–1917?'
- 'How far can the Black Death be considered a turning point in the development of medicine and surgery over the period 1100–1650?'

As you research the turning point you have chosen, remember you will not be looking at what caused the event to happen; you will be looking, instead, for patterns of change across the whole period. In which case, you should be asking: What changed as a result of this event? What stayed the same after this event?

Moderators' notes

It is important to remember that the 'role of individuals' is a factor to be compared to other factors that brought about change. Do not just focus on the individuals. Too many candidates only write a series of mini-biographies. Compare and contrast different factors, the role of the individual included.

Moderators' notes

Researching 'causation' means that as well as focusing on the process of change, you must consider what it was that 'drove' change at this time.

Essential notes

An example of a key factor would be railway development in Britain, 1830–50. It was a key factor in bringing change to Britain's industry. It was one of the reasons why new industries developed and grew.

An example of a key turning point would be the Russian revolution of October 1917. This was a key turning point in the relationship between the Russian state and the peasants. Some things changed and some things stayed the same. It was the same with other possible key turning points, such as the emancipation of the peasants in 1861; some aspects of their life changed and some stayed the same. In this way patterns will be established.

Essential notes

Copy the grid and headings into your file and organise your thinking about your own coursework programme in exactly the same way. Following that, construct two enquiries: one factor-based, and another turning point-based.

Change: causality and patterns

Part B of your assignment focuses on change over the whole of the time period of your coursework programme. Remember that you will investigate this in one of two main ways:

1. By focusing on the significance of a factor (including the role of individuals) in bringing about change. This approach looks specifically at the **causes** of change.

2. By focusing on events as turning points, and thereby determining which one was key in bringing about change. This approach will look at **patterns** of change.

Identifying the two approaches

It is absolutely essential that you are clear about the difference between factor-based and turning point-based enquiries. The tables below are designed to help:

Factor-based enquiries	
Question	Is it asking why something is changing?
Focus	Is it examining causation – the factor(s) that caused change?
Features	Is it asking you to group a range of factors in order of importance so as to show the key cause(s) of change?

Turning point-based enquiries	
Question	Is it asking what changed and what stayed the same?
Focus	Is it examining patterns of change and continuity?
Features	Is it asking you to group a range of events in order of importance so as to show patterns of change and continuity across the whole period and their relative significance in order to determine which patterns were most important?

Deciding which enquiry route to take

In making a decision as to whether to base an enquiry on factors or on turning points, you need first to focus on the process of change that was happening throughout the coursework programme. The following examples illustrate how to decide on which route to take.

Student 1

This student has been following the Edexcel-designed programme CW19: *Representation and Democracy c1830–1931*.

- The student has been thinking about the factors that brought about change during this time, and looking at groups of events in order to identify patterns of change and continuity across the whole of the programme.

- The student has decided to illustrate the findings using a grid as shown.

Factors	What did they bring about?	Turning points	What changed?	What stayed the same?
Popular pressure	1831 Bristol riots → 1832 Reform Act Hyde Park Riots → 1867 Reform Act Militant suffragettes → 1918 Representation of the People Act	1832 Reform Act	Voters increased from 1 in 10 to 1 in 5 56 rotten and pocket boroughs lost their MPs Seats redistributed, mainly to growing industrial towns of the midlands and north.	Electoral corruption Voting not secret Property-owning classes still in control Working classes still could not vote No woman could vote
The aristocracy	Fear of revolution	1911 Parliament Act	Reduced power of House of Lords House of Commons, increased power	Still a House of Lords Titles still awarded by monarch Great tracts of land still owned by the aristocracy
Role of individuals	Votes for women 1867 Reform Act	1872 Secret Ballot Act	Voters could vote in secret	Women still denied the vote Landlords continue to exert some control over voters

The work of Student 1 resulted in two possible enquiries.

- 'Assess the significance of popular pressure in bringing about improved representation and democracy in Britain in the period 1830–1931.'

- 'In considering the process of change in representation and democracy over the whole period 1830–1931, how far can the 1832 Reform Act be considered to be a key turning point?'

Student 2

This student has been following the Edexcel-designed coursework programme CW24: *Medicine in Britain c1870–c1990* and has started a grid.

Factor	What did it bring about?	Turning point	What changed?	What stayed the same?
Technology	X-ray machines Electrocardiographs Heart-lung machines	The First World War	Blood transfusions Skin grafts Brain surgery	Problem of internal infection
Government policies	1911 National Insurance Act 1940 Diphtheria immunisation campaign	NHS Act 1946	Services available to all: free at the point of delivery New salary scale for doctors Nationalisation of hospitals	Family doctors Surgical treatments Drugs Nursing
Role of individuals	Germ theory of disease Discovery of penicillin Heart transplants Aseptic surgery Polio vaccine			

The work of Student 2 resulted in two possible enquiries.
- 'Assess the significance of government policies in bringing about change to medical treatment and surgery in the period 1870–1990.'
- 'To what extent can the First World War (1914–18) be considered to be a key turning point in the process of change in medical treatment and surgery in the years c1870–c1990?'

Change: the relative importance of factors

You have seen how to construct effective titles. You have also looked at how best to construct the two main Part B type enquiries. In doing so, you have learnt: how to identify the difference between factors and turning points, and how to use the strands of a given programme to construct a factor (cause)-based enquiry and a turning point (pattern)-based enquiry.

Now you will focus on the relative importance of factors in bringing about change. You will also be deciding on the degree of weight you give to both the key factor and other factors when following your line of enquiry. In doing so, you will need to:

- look at change across the whole time span of a given programme
- identify the factors that may have contributed to the change
- arrange the factors in order of importance. This will mean looking at how influential each factor is
- decide which factors (key and other) to use in a line of enquiry exploring change
- construct a line of enquiry using the key factor and other factors.

Identifying and ordering the factors

In the course of your studies, you will have identified your coursework's key themes. In doing so, you will have gained a good understanding of the programme's varying processes of change. Now, you need to consider which factors were most influential in terms of causing that change. In thinking about this, you will:

- need to decide on the factor that you believe, from your reading, probably had the most impact on the process of change during your coursework programme
- need to weigh the significance of this factor against other important factors
- make this factor the key factor in your enquiry, while at the same time giving due weight and consideration to the other identified factors.

Example of weighing the significance of a factor

This student is researching change over time in the history of medicine. Their Part B enquiry title is 'Assess the significance of the role of individuals in bringing about change in the development of surgery, 1850–1950.'

The student is going to weigh the importance of the role of individuals against three other factors: government policies, technology and war:

Weighing the factors in Part B: The History of Medicine

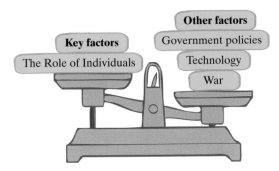

Constructing a factor-based enquiry

It is imperative that you make your key factor the cornerstone of your enquiry. This is the factor that will be in your enquiry title. However, the importance of this key factor is partially defined by how it relates to the other factors you have identified. In which case, you will need to give due weight to these other factors as well.

Time spent on the key factor and other factors in an enquiry

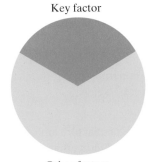

The pie chart clearly shows how much time, thought and space you ought to give to the key factor and to other competing factors. The key factor is given greater weight and consideration than any other individual factor because it is, in your opinion, the most significant factor in driving change within the timeframe of your coursework programme. It is the one factor without which change would not have come about in the way that it did and to the extent that it did.

Analysing factors and their contribution to change

You should aim to spend not less than one third, but not more than half, of your time and available words on analysing your key factor and the contribution it made to the process of change. In what ways, and with what success, did it bring about change? You should then divide the rest of your available words and time in analysing the remaining factors you have chosen. It is important you aren't dealing with too many – three or four would be ideal – because you need to give each one due consideration before you reach your supported judgement.

Moderators' note

Don't make the mistake of focusing totally on just one factor. If you do this, you will ignore discussing other important factors, and so not fully explain how a change occurred. In doing so, you risk either inflating or undermining the importance of the key factor. Giving other significant factors due weight and consideration will help balance your enquiry. Finally, it's unlikely a single factor will be so influential as to be the single cause of change across the whole period.

Change: assessing and contextualising factors

Factors that were important in bringing about change occur in every coursework programme. They will differ from programme to programme. Here are some examples:

You will now look more closely at how to work out – or assess – the relative importance of factors when looking at change across the whole time period of a programme. In doing so, you will also be looking at how best to place the factor(s) in the context of change.

Assessing factors

Lots of factor-based enquiry titles begin with the word 'assess'. In this context, it means that you should evaluate the key factor in relation to the other factors. Look back, for example, at the enquiries into factors that Students 1 and 2 devised on page 19.

Student 1

> 'Assess the significance of popular pressure in bringing about improved representation and greater democracy in Britain in the period 1830–1931.'

Remember, the significance of a factor cannot be properly assessed unless it is compared to other factors that might have been equally significant in bringing about change. Student 1 will therefore have to compare the significance of popular pressure with other factors that brought about change. Look back at Student 1's grid on page 19. It shows that the student:

- has already singled out the role of the aristocracy as an important factor

- believes both the part played by war and the economy to be important.

So, despite identifying popular pressure as the key factor, the student must still consider, evaluate and discuss the role of these other factors in contributing to improved representation and greater democracy in Britain.

Student 2

> 'Assess the significance of government policies in bringing about change to medical treatment and surgery in the period 1870–1990.'

Like Student 1, Student 2 begins the enquiry with the word 'assess'. The student has also identified a handful of significant factors. Look back at Student 2's grid on page 19. The student has selected government policies as the main factor in bringing about change, and the grid shows that the student is aware of the need to compare this with the other identified factors:

- war
- the role of individuals
- technology.

Look back at Student 2's grid on page 19.

Contextualising a factor-based enquiry

When constructing the introduction to a factor-based enquiry, it is vital that you mention both the key factor and the other factors in relation to the change they engendered. In doing so, you contextualise the enquiry.

Look, for example, at how Student 3 below introduces the Part B enquiry into factors that brought about change.

Student 3

The student is following the Edexcel-designed coursework programme CW23: *Colonisation and Decolonisation in Africa, c1870–c1981*. The main focus of this enquiry is 'changing attitudes to Empire in Britain and Africa and the changing ways in which Britain controlled, extended and dismantled its Empire in Africa'.

Below is the title of the enquiry and the student's introduction.

'How far were economic considerations responsible for bringing about the expansion and dismantling of the British Empire in Africa from 1870 to 1981?'

A large part of the continent of Africa fell under Britain's control, exploitation and then abandonment during the years 1870–1981. During this time, Africa was subject to a series of immense transformations. Amid these changes was the exploitation of raw materials and markets, and this led to the theory that economic considerations were the main motives driving the British colonisation and decolonisation of Africa. The change from colonisation to decolonisation, however, highlights other factors leading to the expansion and dismantling of the British Empire in Africa. This enquiry will attempt to shed light on the role of economic considerations as overriding other factors such as nationalism, public opinion and military conflict in the development and destruction of the British Empire in Africa.

Student 3 has written a clear introduction. The student has contextualised the main factor, 'economic considerations', by relating it to the colonisation and decolonisation of Africa. A clear indication has been given that the student is aware that alternative factors – nationalism, public opinion and military conflict – have to be considered before reaching a conclusion.

Moderators' notes

Both students' titles begin with the word 'assess'. It's important to remember that all factor-based enquiries assess the relative importance of factors.

Moderators' notes

'Contextualise' means that you need to show that you understand the historical background, or environment, that surrounds the process of change you are describing and analysing. You need, in other words, to show that you understand the context within which changes are taking place.

Change: the role of individuals as factors

When assessing the influence of individuals in factor-based enquiries, it is important that you understand an individual or group of individuals as another factor. This particular factor is called 'the role of individuals'. Understood in this sense, remember:

- An individual/group of individuals may or may not be an important factor in a given enquiry.

- The number of individuals discussed depends on their importance as a factor.

- The importance of an individual/group of individuals needs to be compared and contrasted with other factors.

Of course, you are entitled, given enough evidence, to argue that 'the role of individuals' is the key factor in terms of influencing change across the whole time span of a programme.

The following introduction by Student 4 to the Edexcel-designed coursework programme CW23: *Colonisation and Decolonisation in Africa, c1870–c1981* does exactly this. Below is the title of the enquiry and the introduction.

Student 4

> **'Assess the significance of the role of individuals in the expansion and collapse of the British Empire 1870–1981.'**
>
> The role of individuals was central to the British colonisation of Africa. For example, Cecil Rhodes, who amassed a fortune by acquiring mining concessions in South Africa, did a great deal to popularise imperialism back in Britain. This was partly responsible for the British 'scramble for Africa', with the British pouring into Africa in search of raw materials and cheap labour to exploit it. As he was in direct contact with the British government, Rhodes was a key player in influencing their actions. Missionaries like David Livingstone tended to impose a cultural domination on Britain's African colonies centred on Christianity, where religion was used to legitimise, sustain and endorse political tyranny and coercion.

> Student 4 is here explaining how specific individuals had a role in the development of colonisation. As an introduction, it is reasonable in that it immediately looks at the key factor in relation to change. However, to be improved the introduction would have to introduce other factors with which to compare and contrast the key factor.

It is difficult to grasp the role of the individual in factor-based enquiries. However, if you view it as a factor, in relation to other factors, everything will fall into place.

Student 5

Consider how Student 5 sums up a factor-based enquiry in the Edexcel-designed coursework programme CW38: *The Making of Modern Russia 1856–1964*. Below is the title of the enquiry and the conclusion.

> **'How significant was the role of individuals in the making of modern Russia in the years 1856–1964?'**
>
> The significance of the role of individuals in the making of modern Russia was considerable. Other factors, such as war and repression made notable contributions, with war a major contributory factor to the revolutions of 1917, and repression providing a vital ingredient in maintaining communist rule. Social groups such as the peasants were of high significance in influencing political policy, and industrialisation made Russia comparable to advanced Western powers. But it was the role of individuals – Trotsky, Lenin, Stalin – for example, which provided the driving force for revolutions and dictated policies for the Soviet Union to follow. This factor above all others was the key to converting a backward nation ruled by a Tsarist autocracy into an industrialised superpower.

Throughout this response, Student 5 has analysed the part played by a range of factors in bringing about change. Here, the student sums up the part played by each, and the inter-relationship between the factors and Russian history. A fine conclusion.

Moderators' notes

You need to plan your analysis carefully. Think first of the argument you are going to make about the importance of the role of the individual. Then decide on the individuals you can use to bring in to support or challenge the argument you are making. You may be using 'the role of individuals' as a key factor, or you may be using it as an alternative factor to the one you think is 'key'. Whichever way you are using it, it is essential that you deal with the 'role of individuals' as a single factor to be compared to alternative factors.

Elizabeth Fry, Horatio Lord Nelson, Florence Nightingale and Martin Luther King.

All these individuals had important parts to play in their time. Their role should be considered along with others who also helped to bring about change at that time.

Edwin Chadwick

Elizabeth Fry

Emmeline Pankhurst

Florence Nightingale

Horatio Nelson

Mao Zedong

Martin Luther King, Jr

Mary Queen of Scots

Moderators' notes

A turning point is an event that marks the beginning of a completely new stage in the development of a specific part of the history of a country or a people. Although elements of continuity will remain, elements of change must be greater.

Turning points: identifying, comparing, using

As you have seen, part of the focus in Part B enquiries is on identifying patterns of change and continuity. Using a simple grid (see page 19), you noted events that you thought might be considered turning points. These events, grouped together, constitute a pattern of change across the whole period of the coursework programme.

You will now consider evaluating the individual significance of turning points. Every time you consider the significance of a turning point, you need to ask the following important questions:

1. What changed as a result of the event?

2. What stayed the same? What, in other words, remained unaffected by the event?

Deciding on your key turning point

Over the course of your studies, you will have gained a working knowledge of the period's patterns of change. As a result, you will have a good idea which events are responsible for change, and which events are responsible for ensuring continuity. Obviously, those events that did not result in change are not considered turning points.

In respect of events that did bring about change, it is important that you assess their significance in relation to the change. To do this, look at each turning point and ask yourself:

• To what extent did change occur as a result of the event: a little, some, or a lot?

• If a lot, then how important was the change across the whole time period? Was it short-lived, long-lasting, or central to the period?

Once done, compare and contrast the significance of each event. Decide which, in your opinion, is the most important. Once identified, it will become your enquiry's key turning point. This whole process is vital to the success of your enquiry.

Working with a turning point

Look, for example, at the enquiry that was considered on page 19:

> 'In considering the process of change in representation and democracy over the whole period 1830–1931, how far can the 1832 Reform Act be considered to be a key turning point?'

Clearly, the key turning point being focused on here is the 1832 Reform Act, and the enquiry will need to assess just how important a stage this was in Britain's road to representation and democracy. However, as seen in the table on page 19, it was not the only turning point identified. There are other contributing events worth considering, a fact hinted at by the title's use of the phrases 'how far' and 'to what extent'. Both these key phrases invite you to speculate as to the overriding importance of the 1832 Reform Act.

In uncovering just how important it was, due weight and consideration must be given to other turning points: to the 1911 Parliament Act, the 1867 Reform Act and the 1928 Representation of the People Act. These turning points will together cover the whole period 1830–1931.

Essential elements of a turning point-based enquiry

So, in any turning point-based enquiry, it is essential that both the key turning point and the other turning points be accorded due weight and consideration. It is essential, too, that the patterns of change and continuity you identify cover the whole period of the coursework programme.

Dividing your time between different turning points

Time spent on the key turning point and other turning points in an enquiry

Key turning point

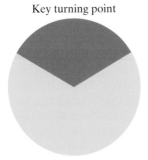

Other turning points

As with the work on factors (see page 21), the above pie chart clearly shows how much time, thought and space you ought to give to the key turning point and to other competing turning points. The key turning point is given greater weight and consideration than any other individual turning point because it is, in your opinion, the most significant one in bringing about change within the timeframe of your coursework programme. It is the one turning point that created the greatest difference in the patterns of change and continuity across the whole period.

You should aim to spend not less than one third, but not more than half, of your time and available words on analysing your key turning point and the impact it had on the patterns of change and continuity across the period. You should then divide the rest of your available words and time in analysing the remaining turning points you have chosen.

It is important you aren't dealing with too many key turning points – three or four would be ideal – because you need to give each one due consideration before you reach your supported judgement.

You will now look at two student answers, and what they have written about their selected turning points.

Moderators' notes

Long periods of change may well have a key turning point, but they are the result of bundles of turning points, all of which are in some way linked to the key turning point. Look carefully at what happened after the identified turning points. Ask yourself what changed, how important that change was, and whether the change was part of a pattern.

Continued on the next two pages

Student 6

The following extract from Student 6 focuses on a key turning point in international relations during the 20th century. The student was following the Edexcel-designed coursework programme CW40: *Twentieth Century International Relations 1879–1980*. Below is the title and an extract from the enquiry:

Essential notes

The attack on Pearl Harbor, Hawaii, occurred in December 1941 when the Japanese airforce attacked the US Pacific fleet on its base. This action brought the USA into the Second World War.

> **'In considering the process of change in relationships between the powers and the way in which this affected the balance of power 1879–1980, how far can Pearl Harbor be seen as a key turning point?'**
>
> The key turning point came on 7th December 1941 at Pearl Harbor – what President Roosevelt declared as a 'day of infamy'. It was the day when 'the war came to America and America came to the war', suggesting that as a result of Japanese aggression, the USA was forced into worldwide conflict. In 'continuing to look inwards' the passing of neutrality Acts in the 1930s, the USA distanced itself from European affairs, especially following internal problems ignited by the Great Depression. However, Pearl Harbor forced America to revert from their isolationist policy to an interventionist one, sparking American involvement in the Second World War, a decision collectively supported by the US population. This marked a turning point in the course of the war with American intervention leading the allied powers to victory in 1945, something that appeared unlikely after Germany's blitzkrieg had swept through the Low Countries and most of Europe. Importantly, Pearl Harbor also represented a political turning point with the emergence of capitalism as the dominant ideology that would confront the communist USSR in the Cold War. Arguably, without Pearl Harbor it would have been Hitler and his totalitarian style ideology that would have surfaced.

Student 6 is exploring the ways in which US intervention in the Second World War as a result of the Japanese attack on the US base at Pearl Harbor was a key turning point in the ways in which it impacted on patterns of change and continuity in international relations. Given America's post-war dominance of international relations, the student is correct to identify it as a key turning point. The argument would have to be supported by comparing the relative significance of other turning points – the Marshall Plan, the atom bomb, the moon landings, Vietnam – for it to be considered really good.

However, not all students discovered that the turning point they originally thought of as being 'key' turned out to be so. The extract below from Student 7 is a response to an enquiry in the Edexcel-designed coursework programme CW7: *Rebellion and Disorder in Tudor England 1485–1587*.

Student 7

'In considering the process of change in political stability in England over the whole period 1485–1584, how far can the Pilgrimage of Grace be seen as a key turning point?'

The Pilgrimage of Grace in 1536 brought with it a threat unmatched in the dynasty, yet one must question whether this insurrection, or, rather, its suppression, can be viewed as the key turning point with regards to the political stability of the nation. Recently, historians have warmed to the belief that the 'Pilgrimage' was an authentic and potentially dangerous expression of Northern discontent against the Henrician regime. Indeed, Dawson and Rex go so far as to say that it was the 'crisis of the reign'. However, if the Pilgrimage is indeed to be perceived as a key political turning point of the era, this would imply that its suppression significantly altered the balance of power within the region, resulting in a Tudor supremacy that was to remain unchallenged for a generation. This was not the case.

Essential notes

The Pilgrimage of Grace (1536) was a series of risings in Lincolnshire and the northern counties of England. The 'pilgrims' were protesting against the dissolution of the monasteries and were staunch supporters of the Catholic faith. The rebels were persuaded to disperse peacefully, but further disturbances in 1537 led to harsh repression by the authorities.

Student 7 is looking at the criteria to be employed if the Pilgrimage of Grace were to be considered a key turning point, and they have decided that it doesn't match up. Their answer must go on to provide evidence to support the point they are making in challenging the views of two historians. Clearly, this is an introduction to the enquiry, and the student's opinion would have to be subsequently supported by a range of secondary sources. However, if it did go on to back opinion with evidence, it would be an excellent answer.

The Pilgrimage of Grace by Fred Kirk Shaw, c. 1913

Moderators' notes

A contemporary source is one written at the time of your enquiry, but not necessarily by people involved in the event

Moderators' notes

A secondary source is one written after the event, often but not always, by a historian. He or she would not have been involved in the event but would be reflecting on it and analysing what happened at a later date.

As a general rule, anything written outside the timeframe of your coursework programme would be a secondary source. When it comes to 20th-century coursework programmes, there will not be very much written outside the coursework programme! Here, it would be sensible to take as a secondary source anything written by a historian, reflecting on events later on.

Essential notes

The author may have separated the sources of evidence into sections: for example, 'Documents', 'Diaries and letters', 'Local studies' and 'Secondary sources'. Alternatively, the author may have listed the sources alphabetically. Either way, if you take the time to familiarise yourself with the book's organisation, you will make the task of finding your own sources that much easier.

Books, magazines and the internet

You will have been taught an overview of the coursework topic you are following, and you will have worked out the Part A and Part B enquiries you are interested in. You may not have finalised these yet, but don't worry. You will now look at three essential sources of information: books, magazines and the internet. Reading up on the topic will help you sort out the exact focus you want.

Books and magazines

Books and magazines are excellent sources for contemporary and secondary source material. However, remember that the Part A and Part B enquiries have different focuses.

Source material for the Part A enquiry

When looking for source material for your Part A enquiry, your focus is on the short-term significance of an individual, event, movement or development. You will need to find:

- Contemporary sources connected with your Part A enquiry, from which you will eventually select between four and six to evaluate.

- Secondary sources designed to either support or challenge the contemporary source material you are thinking of using.

Source material for the Part B enquiry

When looking for source material for your Part B enquiry, remember your focus is on the process of change across the whole time period of a coursework programme. You will need to find secondary sources that will give you information, insight and opinions relating to the question you have chosen for your Part B enquiry.

Focusing your research

At first, the task of having to find enough source material may seem a challenge. If you break it down into small steps, you will find it becomes manageable.

Starting point: a single book

One of the most sensible starting points would be the book that first interested you in the topic(s) that is the subject of your enquiry. It may have been a textbook written specifically for your coursework programme or it may be a book that focuses on just part of that programme. Either way, it should be a book that gives a simple overview of your area of interest. Easy to read, more lightweight than detailed academic study, it is a resource that will lead you to find other sources. When reading it, look for:

- The bibliography. This will list the sources the author used when writing the book. If you are lucky, these will be separated into contemporary and secondary sources. If not, you will have to do this yourself.

- Footnotes. Situated at the foot of each page, these can also lead you to other documents, articles and books. Some authors use them to provide authors and titles of books referred to on the page. Others use them to clarify points made or to provide additional information.

- Endnotes. Situated either at the end of a chapter or the book, these serve the same purpose as footnotes. However, they can be more detailed, and will sometimes give valuable insights into the author's opinions and research techniques.
- Quotations. When reading the main text, you will find quotations that you might think relevant to your enquiry. The author should have indicated where they came from.

Researching journals and magazines

Articles in journals and magazines can be very helpful in focusing on a specific aspect of a historical topic. They can give fresh insights and new and up-to-date ideas.

The magazines that would probably be of most use to you are:

- *History Review*
- *BBC History Magazine*
- *History Today.*

They all contain articles and features on different aspects of British, European and World History, from the earliest times to the 21st century. Browse through them in your local newspaper shop or library, and see which ones suit you best in style and approach. They all have online indexes, and it would be sensible, too, to consult these so that you can see the range and type of article offered, and whether or not there are any that relate directly to your coursework programme.

Organising your reading

As you read, you will come across more and more relevant source material.

It is essential that you write down the references to the source material. Initially, this will be a 'this interests me' list of authors' names, books, historical figures, references to quotes, books and magazines. Remember, the references on this first list may or may not actually be used in your enquiry. However, as the list grows, and you become much more certain of the sources you will use, you will need to organise your research notes.

- Disregard the sources that have nothing to do with your enquiry.
- Transfer the notes you consider relevant to the enquiry to a 'likely to use' list. You should keep this list in your resource record (see pages 64–7).
- Separate references to contemporary sources from references to secondary sources. You may find it useful to use a system of grids such as the examples on the next page. You should construct two grids, one for references to contemporary material and the other for references to secondary source material. Remember that contemporary sources are only useful for your Part A enquiry.
- Write a short comment beside each of your reference to sources notes. This will act as an *aide memoire*, and it will make the job of constructing your enquiry that much easier.

For an example of a student's 'likely to use list', please see the next two pages.

Essential notes

The journal/magazine titles listed here are just three of the most widely available magazines. There are many others that you could consult.

Essential notes

When making your lists, do not copy out quotes or great tracts of secondary evidence. Instead, with secondary sources make a note of the author, title, page number and publication date. Do the same for contemporary sources, except replace the publication date with the actual year of the source. If it is a journal or a magazine, make a note of the issue number.

☞ **Continued on the next four pages**

This student is following a centre-designed coursework programme *Public Health and Welfare 1830–1950*. The student has started collecting references to sources that might be used. Here is the 'likely to use' list:

Secondary sources

Author	Title	ISBN/publication date	Comments
Norman Longmate	King Cholera	Published 1966 No ISBN	Specific to cholera
Roy Porter	The Greatest Benefit to Mankind	Published 1999 ISBN 0-00-215173-1	Looks to be very general. Maybe a chapter on public health?
Stephen Halliday	The Great Stink of London	Published 1999 ISBN 0-7509-1975-2	Specific to public health?

Contemporary sources

Author	Title	Date	Comments
J.A. Lawrie	Essays on Cholera in Sunderland, Newcastle and Gateshead	1832	Might be worth looking for, particularly if believes in miasma theory
John Snow	On the Mode of Communication of Cholera	1849	Must find – central to my Part A because his research showed cholera was a water-borne disease. Shows short-term significance of ...

You have now organised your research using a single coursework book and/or well-known magazines as a starting point. You will have made a list of titles, authors and publication dates along with references to source material you would like to research. You now need to know where best to find the material, in particular using the internet and 'real-world' libraries and resource centres.

The internet

In terms of researching your enquiry, the internet is an indispensable tool. However, it is also a vast and unregulated space. Be aware:

- There is a huge amount of information that will be relevant to the topics you are following. While you may be able to find more material on the internet than at your local library, a glut of source material such as that provided by online websites can waste valuable research time.

- Unlike 'real-world' sources (books, journals and magazines), a lot of the material on the internet remains unedited. Unedited material may be the work of a lone blogger. It may appear on a single-issue website, or in the sales-driven pages of a business. It could be the result of conversations held in interest-led chat rooms. It could even be 'spoofed' material.

Clearly, the internet needs to be used carefully. If you are going to use it – and we suggest you do – it is essential that you use reputable websites, and that you cross-reference any information found.

Searching the internet

When searching the internet, it is important that you understand why website addresses end in a range of different ways. Normally abbreviations, these endings – suffixes – relate to the nature of the domain owner of the website. Some domains are owned by private individuals, some by private bodies or corporations and some by public organisations (see right).

Researching using the internet

Reputable websites

As a rule of thumb, government and large organisations will have a system of checks and balances with regards to information posted on their sites. Private individual sites are not subject to the same scrutiny. This is not to say that the information on them is necessarily any less reliable than the information on, say, a .org site, but a site managed by an organisation is more likely to have been checked by someone other than the person posting the information.

So, in deciding what to trust, ask yourself the following questions:

- Is the website an official online outlet for a reputable 'real-world' publication? Most journals and magazines are now online, and lots of books have been digitalised. Check.

- What is the purpose of the website? Is it there to inform, explain, persuade or attack? Is the tone alarmist, exaggerated? Is it calm and balanced?

- Who is the author? Is the author qualified to write about the subject? Is he or she, for example, an established academic or a journalist with expertise in the field? If there is no author's name, then can you find out who published the material? If there is no indication as to provenance, then be aware that no one is making themselves accountable for the views expressed on the site.

- Is the site up-to-date? Some websites are updated regularly. Some may have been untouched for years, the material on them hopelessly dated.

- What links are provided? A good site will provide you with links to other sites that provide evidence to back up what they are saying. Test those links.

Essential notes

A suffix is a letter or group of letters that is added at the end of a word or, in this case, a website address:

- **.gov** indicates that the site is a government website and so the material is published by an official organisation
- **.org** indicates that the site is run by a non-profit-making organisation
- **.edu** indicates that the site is run by an educational organisation
- **.com** indicates that the site has been bought by a commercial organisation

If you come across a website address with the name of a person in it, or the words 'members' or 'users', then be aware that these sites are privately managed.

Essential notes

Wikipedia is a helpful resource. An online, self-regulated encyclopedia, it is regularly updated, checked and commented on, and intends to provide unbiased information. Even so, you should be aware that anyone can contribute to it, whether or not they have specialist knowledge. Most importantly, access is not restricted to the domain holders, and material can be temporarily added to or removed. It is best used as a springboard for more detailed research.

☞ **Continued on the next two pages**

'Real-world' libraries and resource centres

All schools and colleges have libraries, and you may be lucky enough to live close to a public library. Some libraries are called resource centres because they provide you with other resources apart from books. These resources, such as audio recordings or microfilms, usually have to be booked in advance. Access to books does not!

A modern resource centre (source: British Library © Andrew Dunn)

Books classified according to the Dewey Decimal System

Looking for books and related resources

There are three ways to find the information you are looking for:

1. The library's electronic search engine. This is useful if you know the author, the title or the ISBN of the book, journal, audio-visual material or microfiche you want. It is also useful for more general searches. The search engine will tell you if the library has a copy, if it is available to borrow and whether copies are available in nearby libraries. It will give you a number according to the Dewey Decimal System of Classification.

2. The library's physical catalogue. This is useful if you know the author of the book you want. Libraries list all their books alphabetically, with the author's surname coming first and then the title of the book. The catalogue will tell you whether or not the library holds a copy of the book you are looking for, and where it can be found. It will give you a number according to the Dewey Decimal System.

3. Dewey Decimal System of Classification. This is the standard classification system used by the majority of libraries. The system organises books by subject and then by topic within that subject. You could, therefore, start with the Dewey Decimal Classification to get to the subject area you are looking for.

Looking for local history

County record offices and libraries in most major cities and towns have local studies departments. You can usually find out online what sorts of records they hold. Their collections usually contain maps and plans, newspapers, photographs and posters, records of local companies, school log books and petitions. Once you have found out the sort of contemporary sources you are looking for in connection with your Part A enquiry, it would be sensible to make an appointment to see the archivist in charge to talk through what it is you are looking for. The example below shows how one student went about it:

This student is working on the Edexcel-designed coursework programme CW27: *Challenging Authority: from Corresponding Societies to the Poll tax 1789–1992*, where the focus is the objectives and methods of protest in the period, the response of authority and the extent to which protest was successful.

For the Part A enquiry, the student is thinking of researching the short-term impact of the repeal of the Combination Acts in 1824. An internet trawl revealed that the local studies library in Bradford held records that might be of interest and the student made an appointment to see the local archivist and explore what records they had. The student found a letter from Henry Carter, a Halifax mill-owner, to Mr W Moulden, a Bradford solicitor acting for the mill-owners:

An example of contemporary evidence

> Lightcliffe
> Nr Halifax
>
> Sept 3rd 1825
> Sir
> In answer to the circular I have recd. from you, I wd beg to say that the few workpeople I employ are chiefly elderly men and their families who have been employed under me nearly all their lives. I apprehend they do not belong to, nor are connected with any club or union, nor have they shown the least disposition for an advance of wages. Shd such circumstances take place in the present situation of Trade, I feel it my duty to unite with the general body of Manufacturers in resisting their demands.
> I remain, Sir, your most obt. Serv.
> John Carter
> If any of my men be in this Union I shall certainly discharge them.
> Henry Carter

Essential notes

The repeal of the Combination Acts in theory made trades unions legal. The repeal was followed by a wave of strikes. The strikes were partly caused by a trade boom, which made the strikers believe that their employers could afford to pay them more, but the employers blamed the repeal of the Combination Acts and the increase in union activity.

Here was excellent contemporary evidence of the attitude of those in authority to protest and strikes. The student will need to interrogate the source, making links between the Bradford solicitor and the circular he sent to all mill owners, and the attitude shown by this particular mill owner to his employees.

Note-taking and note-making

Note-taking and note-making is best approached methodically. If you are organised from the beginning you will:

- save time
- remain consistent
- record information accurately
- have all the information with which to write up your assignment.

It is important, therefore, that you have a note-taking and note-making system that works for you. An efficient system should include:

Keeping your notes efficiently

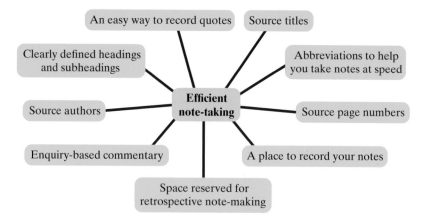

Where to make your notes

You will have been making notes throughout the course, and should – by the time you begin focusing on a piece of enquiry-led research – know what works best for you.

Possible places to make and keep notes

Whichever system you use, it is essential that it is flexible. Make sure your system can cope with amendments without becoming impossible to understand.

Before making notes

If you are taking notes from a secondary source, you should note down the author, title, publisher and date of publication. For example:

> Alan Farmer, *The Origins of the American Civil War 1846–61* (published by Hodder & Stoughton, 2002)

If you are working with a contemporary source, you should note where you found it. For example:

> Newsletter from Leith 24 April 1652, published in Toby Barnard, *The English Republic* (published by Longman, 1982)

Once you have done this, you can begin making notes.

When making notes

Unless you are recording a quote, avoid writing your notes in longhand. Apart from saving time, abbreviated notes are easier to locate and therefore use. There are some universally recognised symbols and abbreviations that you could use.

Symbol/ abbreviation	What it means	Symbol/ abbreviation	What it means
∴	therefore	∵	because
NB	literally, *nota bene*, which is Latin for 'note well'	→	leading to
<	less than	>	greater than

You can also shorten some words so that you write less but what you do write is still clear. For example:

Shortened word	Word	Shortened word	Word
gov	government	rev	revolution
MLK	Martin Luther King	ind	industry/ industrial
parl	parliament	Opp	opposition

In addition to abbreviating your notes, do not forget to organise them using headings and subheadings. This will ensure that they are clear and accessible. A heading, therefore, should indicate a topic, while a subheading should break the topic into manageable chunks.

Finally, when making notes of quotes you want to use, do not use shorthand. Either write up the quote in longhand or photocopy the relevant page, highlight the quote and add to your notes. Always give the full title, author and page number in case you need to check it again. The example on the next page shows how one student went about it.

Essential notes

In addition to making sure you've taken down the author, title, publisher and date of publication, remember to make a note of the page number of the book. This will save time if you need to:

- return to the source for more information
- acknowledge the source in your enquiry's endnotes.

Essential notes

You could always develop your own set of abbreviations, but be consistent: you will need to remember what they are. Also, remember you must not use abbreviations when you write up your assignment.

☞ Continued on the next two pages

Student 1

This student is following the Edexcel-designed coursework programme CW21: *Britain and India 1845–1947*. Below is an extract from the book the student is reading, along with the student's notes on the book details and content.

> **Lawrence James, *Raj: The Making and Unmaking of British India* (published by Little, Brown and Company, 1997 p558)**
>
> Domestic opposition to Indian independence was muted and confined to right-wing Conservatives, with Churchill uttering sibylline warnings about Britain's decline as a world power. The old arguments that Britain needed India no longer carried much weight. It was pointless to regard the Indian army as the bulwark for British power in Asia at a time when Indian politicians and some soldiers were vehemently protesting against the deployment of Indian forces in Indonesia and Indo-China, where they were upholding Dutch and French imperial pretensions. There were no British settlers in India, as there were in southern Africa, who could rally support in Parliament. Most important of all, India had ceased to be a commercial asset of any kind.

Student 1's notes

> Indian Indep.
>
> Opp in GB to indep = rt wing Cons eg Churchill afraid → decline of GB as world pwr.
> NB   Br settlers in India not rallying anti- independence support in Parl
> BUT
> (i)   Indian army no longer reliable support for GB in Asia
> (ii)   India no longer commercial asset to GB
>
> → collapse of old arguments re GB need for India

Essential notes

It is true that only you have to read your own notes. It is important, however, that they make sense to you, even weeks later. So don't be too brief and don't use abbreviations that later you may wonder about.

An alternative way of making your notes

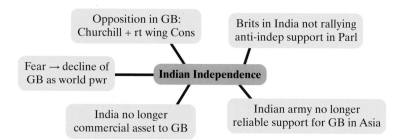

Student 1's abbreviated notes	The meaning of the abbreviations
Indian Indep.	Indep = independence
Opp in GB to indep = rt wing Cons eg Churchill afraid → decline of GB as world pwr.	Opp = opposition GB = Great Britain rt = right eg = example pwr = power
NB Br settlers in India not rallying anti-independence support in Parl	NB = *nota bene* (Italian for 'note well') Br = Britain Parl = parliament
BUT (i) Indian army no longer reliable support for GB in Asia ii) India no longer commercial asset to GB	GB = Great Britain
→ collapse of old arguments re GB need for India	→ = leading to

This is a good piece of note-making. The student has teased out the essential elements from quite a tricky passage. The notes the student has made relate directly to the programme's main theme. They are easy to follow, contain a wealth of information and should contribute to the assignment.

Making notes electronically

Some students prefer to make their notes electronically, using iPads, laptops or other electronic devices. This is, of course, perfectly acceptable. Whatever you use has to be convenient for you and appropriate for the place where you will be taking notes. Your bedroom at home, for example, may be the perfect place to make notes on your laptop, whilst librarians in a public library might not be very happy with you doing this. There are three factors you must bear in mind when using electronic devices:

1. Do not persuade yourself that electronic devices are automatically better because you like using them: be realistic about which method really works best for you.

2. If you are using a range of different methods of note-taking – for example, handwritten on cards and on a laptop – make sure that you bring them all together. There must be a central point where they are all assembled, otherwise you'll spend a lot of time searching for notes you know you have made but can't quite find.

3. Back up! Electronic devices, no matter how apparently sound and reliable, do crash. So make sure you back up on an external hard drive, CD-ROM or memory stick.

Essential notes

Remember, in the event that you come across quotations you think may come in use when writing up your assignment, make sure you either copy them out in longhand, or photocopy and highlight the relevant passage(s). Don't forget to note down where the quotation comes from – and the page number.

Moderators' notes

Your reading of secondary sources will provide the background and the context into which you will need to fit your evaluation of contemporary sources. You will not be evaluating the secondary sources.

Using secondary sources as a resource

By this stage in your coursework planning, you will have a very good idea of what the focus of your Part A enquiry will be, and you will have collected references to a range of secondary and contemporary sources.

As you move through the following pages you will be learning how to use a variety of source materials as a resource with which to support your Part A enquiry. They are:

- contemporary written sources (see page 46)
- contemporary pictorial sources (see page 48)
- artefacts and archaeological finds (see page 50)
- secondary sources (see page 54).

Starting off: reading around the subject using secondary sources

You will have been taught an overview of the coursework programme, and so you will have a good idea of what happened when, and what the main issues were. Also, you will have by now chosen the subject of your Part A enquiry. Now you need to do some reading around the enquiry. This is for three main reasons:

1. You need to find out the background to the topic you have chosen.
2. You need to discover which specific issues – relating to this topic – are important.
3. You need to make sure that you know exactly how the contemporary sources you have chosen fit into the history of the period that you will learn about from reading secondary sources. You will need to be sure of how these contemporary sources relate to and develop the issues you have identified in your reading.

Make notes on the above three points. You could use the following subheadings: Background, Main issues, How my contemporary sources relate to enquiry's background and issues.

Remember, when reading around a topic, do not read the whole book. Scan it. Look at what the title of your enquiry is asking you to do. Concentrate on the background, the issues and the contemporary source material that relates to the enquiry. Refine your research techniques:

- use the book's contents page to find relevant information
- use its index to find names, dates and events
- if necessary, read the introductory chapter to give you an overview of the book's content
- if necessary, read the concluding chapter to find out the author's final thoughts.

Of course, if you find a book particularly interesting, and have the time, then by all means read all of it. However, when researching the background to an enquiry, use a book as a resource and take from it only what you need. The example opposite shows how one student went about it.

Student 1

This student is following the Edexcel-designed coursework programme CW7: *Rebellion and Disorder in Tudor England 1484–1587*. The student has chosen the following title as the Part A enquiry:

'How significant were the actions taken by Thomas Cromwell in strengthening royal authority in the short term?'

The student is starting with the book *The Tudor Years*, edited by John Lotherington and published by Hodder & Stoughton in 1994. The book consists of a series of sections, each one written by an academic historian.

This is what the student does:

1. Goes to the contents pages at the beginning of the book. The student will need to read up about the reign of Henry VIII, which was the time when Thomas Cromwell was working.

2. Discovers that there are three sections on Henry VIII, written by two different historians. The student feels a bit daunted at the prospect of having to read and take notes from over 100 pages.

3. Decides to use the index at the back of the book. This shows exactly where in the book there are references to Thomas Cromwell. By cross-referencing between the index and the contents page, the student can focus on those pages where reading and notes are really needed.

Extracts from the contents and index pages used by Student 1

Essential notes

An academic historian is one working in a university. This kind of historian normally specialises in a particular subject. If the subject is broad, then he or she will usually specialise in an aspect of the topic.

Finding and using relevant contemporary sources

By now you will have located a number of contemporary sources that could be relevant to your Part A enquiry. However, you may have made a note of a lot of contemporary sources; you may feel slightly overwhelmed by what you have and you may be unsure as to how to select useful sources. Do not worry. Consider the following:

- Are the sources truly contemporary to the period? If they are, then they could be of use.

- Is there a good range of source material? If so, then they will help make and shape the enquiry.

- Do the sources support and develop the issues raised from reading about the topic? If yes, then they will help deepen the enquiry.

These basic questions will help reduce the number of contemporary sources. They will also improve the quality of your collection. The section below shows you in detail how they help do this.

Finding a good range of contemporary sources

As you think about and respond to each of these three questions, you will probably need to discard some of the contemporary sources you have collected. At the end of this process, you will probably be left with a handful of sources that were all created within the right timeframe, are different from each other, and relate well to the issues you have already identified. Look at what Student 2 and Student 3 have done.

Student 2

This student is following the Edexcel-designed coursework programme CW21: *Britain and India 1845–1947*. The focus of the programme is the changing attitudes to empire in Britain and in India, and the changing ways in which Britain controlled and dismantled its empire in India. Student 2's Part A enquiry and the sources selected to work with are shown below:

Moderators' notes

'Range' means a number of different types of sources. These may be written sources, such as legal documents, official records, private letters, diaries, poems and newspaper articles and reports; they may be pictorial sources, such as paintings, photographs and cartoons; or they may be artefacts, such as statues, coins, tools and even whole buildings.

Essential notes

The massacre took place in the Punjab city of Amritsar on 13 April 1919. Fifty British Indian army soldiers, led by Brigadier-General Dyer, fired on an unarmed gathering of men, women and children without warning.

'What was the short-term significance of the Amritsar massacre of 1919?'

1. Proclamation read out in Amritsar on 13 April 1919 forbidding meetings of any kind.

2. General Dyer's report to his superior officer, General William Beynon, which he received on 14 April 1919.

3. Photograph of British soldiers enforcing the 'crawling order'.

4. An illuminated address presented to General Dyer from the ladies of the Punjab, praising him for the part he played at Amritsar.

5. Speech in Parliament by Edwin Montagu, Secretary of State for India, 8 July 1919.

6. A letter written by Rabindranath to his family in July 1920, reporting on the debates in Parliament, which he had attended.

7. Cartoon by David Low, printed in the Daily News on 16 December 1919.

8. The Hunter Committee report on the massacre, published in May 1920.

9. The report on the massacre from the Indian National Congress Punjab Sub-Committee published in February 1920.

10. R.E.H. Dyer Army Disturbances in the Punjab published in 1920.

Student 3

This student is following the Edexcel-designed coursework programme CW22: *The Changing Role of Women 1850–1950*. The focus of the programme is the changing role and status of women at work and in the home, and the factors driving that change. Student 3's Part A enquiry and the sources selected to work with are shown below:

'What was the short-term significance of the suffragettes 1903–1914?'

1. Emmeline Pankhurst *My Own Story* published in 1914.

2. A photograph of 'Women's Sunday' held in Hyde Park on 21 June 1908.

3. A poster supporting the WSPU's propaganda campaign for the general election of 1910.

4. A cartoon published in the magazine *Punch* in November 1911.

5. An article in *The Suffragette* published 25 October 1912 entitled 'Emmeline Pankhurst at the Albert Hall'.

6. The opinion of the medical journal *The Lancet* on forced feeding, published in August 1912.

7. An eye-witness account of Emily Davison's death at the 1913 Derby.

8. A song *The March of the Women* composed by Dame Ethel Smyth in 1911.

9. Part of a speech by the Home Secretary, Reginald Mckenna in the House of Commons on 11 June 1914.

10. WSPU's *Annual Report* published in 1914.

Essential notes

The suffragettes were a group of women, usually members of the Women's Social and Political Union, who wanted the right to vote on equal terms with men. They grew more and more militant in their activities in the years 1903–14.

Narrowing down your selection of sources

Both students have selected a good range of source material, but they each have too many to evaluate in the extent available (about 2000 words) so will have to narrow down their selection to about five. They do this by assessing the impact the sources are likely to have on the issues raised by their enquiries. Look at the grids on page 44 to see what they put in their final selection, and why. When you come to narrow down your selection of sources, you'll find it useful to use the headings shown in the grid.

☞ Continued on the next two pages

Moderators' notes

Both students have chosen sources that address a number of different issues. They have both selected a good range of different types of source, too.

Student 2: final selection of sources

Source	Issues raised/developed
1. Photograph of British soldiers enforcing the 'crawling order'	Issue: the attitude of the British Army to Indian people
2. Illuminated address presented to General Dyer	Issue: attitude of British citizens living in India, to develop and support Source 1
3. Cartoon by David Low December 1919	Issue: attitude of British public/public opinion/newspapers. To be cross-referenced to Sources 1, 2 and 5
4. Report on massacre published by Indian National Congress February 1920	Issue: impact on Indian attitudes, and for cross-referencing with Source 5 for support and Sources 1 and 2 for contrast
5. Hunter Commission Report on massacre May 1920	Issue: hardening of colonial attitudes: a development of Sources 1 and 2
6. Letter written by Rabindandrath to his family July 1920	Issue: hardening of Indian attitudes and a development of Source 4

Student 3: final selection of sources

Source	Issues raised/developed
1. Extract from Emmeline Pankhurst 'My Own Story' published 1914	Issue: reasons for militancy
2. Photograph of Women's Sunday June 1908	Issue: mass support of men and women; peaceful
3. Poster supporting WSPU's propaganda campaign for the general election of 1910	Issue: impact of suffragettes on politics and public opinion + development to issue of force feeding
4. Cartoon published in *Punch* November 1911	Issue: contrast between suffragettes and suffragists and impact on politics; cross-reference with Source 3
5. Eye-witness account of death of Emily Davison 1913	Issue: commitment of suffragettes and development of propaganda, cross-referenced to Source 3
6. Speech in House of Commons by Reginald McKenna, Home Secretary June 1914	Issue: attitude of government to suffragettes; cross-referenced with Source 4 and developed from that.

An example of a pro-women's suffrage propaganda poster

VOTES

HANDICAPPED!

Using contemporary sources

The sources you finally select will need to be interrogated, evaluated and used in their historical context.

As you work through each source, you will need to do the following.

Identify the source's historical context

- Whereabouts, in the history you have explored with relation to your Part A enquiry, does this source fit in?

- What are the values and assumptions of the society from which it is drawn?

- How typical is it of the society from which it comes?

Interrogate the source as to its nature, origin and purpose

The nature, origin and purpose of a source are all interlinked. For example, you will need to 'listen' to the source, reading between the lines. Is its tone calming or strident, informative and balanced, or displaying one point of view? The origin of the source is closely linked to its nature and purpose.

> **Moderators' notes**
>
> All different types of sources can be interrogated using 'nature, origin and purpose' as the basic questions. They may, however, lead to more questions in-depth.

Using nature, origin and purpose to evaluate the source

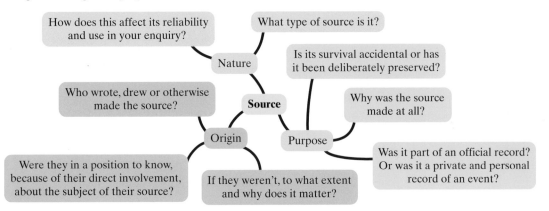

Relate the source to the enquiry

- What issues does the source raise that are related to your enquiry?

- What light does it shed on the short-term significance of your subject?

Ask the above questions of all kinds of sources

All the above questions have to be asked of any source you use: written sources (see page 46), pictorial sources, cartoons, photographs (see page 48), artefacts (see page 50).

☞ **Continued on the next two pages**

Essential notes

The 1832 Reform Act redistributed parliamentary seats so that the growing industrial towns of the midlands and north were represented in parliament. It also extended the franchise so that one man in five could vote in general elections.

Using contemporary written sources

Consider the following examples of two students using contemporary written sources in a Part A enquiry. Refer to the mark schemes on pages 122–5 as you read the moderators' comments.

Student 4: level 1 response

The student is commenting here on a letter written by the Duke of Wellington to a former MP, John Wilson Croker, dated 6 March 1833.

> **'What was the short-term impact of the 1832 Parliamentary Reform Act?'**
>
> The Duke of Wellington was leader of the Tories and the government he led had been defeated in 1830. He had always opposed any reform of parliament. Because this is a private letter, it must be expressing his true feelings. He says that a revolution is made and that power has been transferred from one class to another. He says that democracy is everywhere and no place is safe from it. From my own knowledge I know that this is not totally the case. Before the 1832 Reform Act, one in ten men had the vote; afterwards, it was one in five. So Wellington may have been exaggerating because he was bitterly disappointed that the Act had been passed.

This is a level 1 response to this source. The student has correctly identified the historical context of the letter, but has not used it to develop or raise any issues concerning the reform of parliament at that time. The fourth and fifth sentences are simply paraphrasing the source, which is not necessary.

There is some very limited source evaluation in the third sentence, where the student is assuming that because the letter is a private one, it must be expressing Wellington's true feelings. This, however, is contradicted in the final sentence where the candidate says Wellington may be exaggerating.

There is some cross-referencing with the student's own knowledge regarding the changes to the franchise.

Taken overall, this response is really just a series of simple statements about the source with very little development. The source is related to its historical context. The concept of reliability is addressed, but in a somewhat contradictory way, and the judgements made are stereotypical.

Student 5: level 4 response

The student opposite is commenting on the speech made by US President Roosevelt on 8 December 1941, immediately after Japan's attack on the US naval base at Pearl Harbor.

'What was the short-term significance of Pearl Harbor for international relations in the years up to 1945?'

The decision to place the USA in a state of war with Japan was reflected and, on the face of it, initiated by President Roosevelt's address to America in December 1941. Roosevelt's speech, containing both power and substance, was ignited by the first line 'a day that will live in infamy' and explicitly contemplated the significance of the event for the future of the USA. With frequent references to the impact on the country 'understand the implications to the very life and safety of our nation', Roosevelt makes obvious his desire to extinguish the threat of Japanese aggression, firstly to preserve the safety of America and secondly to allow the allied powers to emerge victorious. Roosevelt's frequent use of personal pronouns such as 'our' and 'we' directly and collectively refer to the American population, helping rouse patriotism and unite the American population. The motives behind the speech could be numerous: an attempt to reassure, to motivate and crucially to mobilise support for the imminent war. In addressing the entire country, the content may have been exaggerated in order to fulfil purposes of motivation, especially at a time of great uncertainty for the American people. The speech appears to be a deliberate response, in this time of uncertainty, to appease the public. Ultimately all these factors attempt to justify America's entrance into the war. This source is dependable as it accurately summarises the emotions that the majority of American's were feeling at this time and implies the extent to which America would go to gain revenge.

This is a level 4 response to this source. The student is interrogating the source by considering its nature, origin and purpose in a confident way. The source is placed in its historical context, and the issues this raises are well explored and explained. The student identifies the purpose of the source, and the motives of Roosevelt in writing and delivering it, which were to prepare the American people for war and to leave them in no doubt that the US government had no choice in the matter.

The student supports this by analysing the way in which the language is used in the source. In the final sentence, the student is cross-referencing with their own knowledge of the American people's reaction to the attack on Pearl Harbor. The source is interrogated confidently and critically in order to identify issues and make judgements. The interpretation and evaluation of the evidence takes account of the nature of the source. The student shows the need to explore the implications of the evidence in the light of its historical context and in the context of the values and assumptions of the society from which it is drawn.

Essential notes

In December 1941, the Japanese airforce attacked the US Pacific fleet that was anchored in its base of Pearl Harbor, Hawaii. This attack brought the USA into the Second World War.

Moderators' notes

The difference between the two responses is stark. The first response (Student 4) does not attempt to consider the evidence in relation to the issues raised by Wellington's letter. In doing so, it fails to relate the source to the enquiry in a meaningful way. The second response (Student 5) does the opposite. It interrogates Roosevelt's speech in relation to the event, and relates the evidence to the enquiry's purpose: assessing the significance of Pearl Harbor in relation to international relations. It is vital that you do the same.

☞ **Continued on the next two pages**

Using contemporary pictorial sources

Some of the contemporary sources you will be using will be pictorial ones. Pictorial sources can provide a rich area to investigate as part of your research and often shed interesting and informative light on a particular investigation. Pictorial sources could include photographs, paintings, cartoons and posters.

Consider the following examples of two students using pictorial sources in a Part A enquiry.

Montgomery bus boycott of 1955 (published in the USA in 1956, Herblock Cartoon, copyright by The Herb Block Foundation)

"Tote Dat Barge! Lift Dat Boycott! Ride Dat Bus!"

Student 6: level 2 response

The student is here commenting on a cartoon, published in 1956, about the bus boycott in Montgomery, Alabama, USA.

> **'How far did the Montgomery Bus Boycott improve equality for black people and the views of white people towards blacks 1955–1965?'**
>
> This cartoon shows the effect the boycott had on bus companies and highlights a reason that the laws eventually changed. Before the boycott, the majority of bus riders were black. This means that during the boycott, bus companies were losing a lot of money. The image of an angry white bus manager losing his temper at a black man simply walking away shows how much it affected the bus companies. This cartoon could be suggesting that a change in laws was inevitable with bus officials becoming increasingly frustrated with the lack of income. However, this still shows that white people in general didn't support black people because they are only worried about losing money, not the rights of 'Negroes'. While taking away the profits of bus managers would help blacks become more equal, it wouldn't change the attitudes of white people. If anything, bus managers would be annoyed with blacks and think they are being a nuisance for not riding the bus, not thinking that they deserve equal rights. This is a problem with the boycott. Many whites who agree with segregation and that whites are superior will think that blacks were causing trouble and dislike them more.

This is a level 2 response to this source. The student is relating the cartoon to its historical context, but this is not developed. The student is describing its content and is beginning to explain its meaning. Simple inferences are drawn about what the cartoon could be suggesting – that a change in the law was inevitable. However, the student does not explain why the cartoon was made. In this respect, the student fails to interrogate the evidence, its purpose, the motivations behind its publication. The student ends by reflecting on the boycott itself and as to whether it might increase animosity between blacks and whites. Although this could be seen as an attempt to further contextualise the cartoon, the student presents no evidence for this. In doing so, the student is opened up to charges of speculation, and the student's argument – right or wrong – is thus easily refuted. The source is interpreted beyond its surface features and related to its historical context. Some attention is paid to the source's nature, origin and purpose when addressing concepts such as utility and reliability.

Student 7: level 3 response

The student is here commenting on Michelangelo's painting *Doni Tondo*.

> **'How significant was Michelangelo in the years 1498–1508 for Renaissance art, thought and politics?'**
>
> The *Doni Tondo* or *Doni Madonna* was probably commissioned by Agnolo Doni to commemorate his marriage to Maddalena Strozzi, the daughter of a powerful Tuscan family. The painting is in the form of a Tondo, or round frame, which is frequently associated during the Renaissance with domestic ideas.
>
> However, this cannot be described as a typical Renaissance painting. Technically, the painting is revolutionary. Michelangelo's technique includes shading from the most intense colours first to the lighter shades on top, using the dark colours as shadows, a technique called *cangiante*. By applying pigment in a certain way, Michelangelo created an unfocused effect in the background and detail in the foreground. Mary's torso is twisted reaching for the baby Christ, her body shown at an awkward angle. This demonstrated movement in a far more superior way than was being shown at the time: this was an unconventional portrait of Mary. Contemporary criticism was not only due to the unique treatment of the holy family, but the nudes in the background and John the Baptist in the middle ground of the painting caused a minor uproar and unrest. Michelangelo himself considered such criticisms small-minded and unimportant as the imagery used in the painting symbolised the transition from the pagan age to the Christian age with the birth of Jesus. This shows, again, how Michelangelo was a pioneer in improving the artists' status from that of craftsman to one answerable only to his own creative intuition.

Doni Tondo, painted by Michaelangelo in 1504

This is a level 3 response to this source. The student begins by explaining the origins of the source – the reasons it was created. The historical context explained, the student confidently outlines the technical and material aspects of the painting in relation to Michelangelo's revolutionary approach. In doing so, the student clearly relates the painting, its creator and subject, to the enquiry. In describing Mary's torso, and the fact of John the Baptist's presence, the student demonstrates understanding of the need to interpret sources in the light of the values of the society from which the evidence is drawn. However, the student fails to capitalise on the insight. The student needs to have further explored the artist's impact by comparing the painting with other Michelangelo works. This way, the student would have been able to build a case in support of the argument. The student could have shown that the painting is part of a general approach, and that its commission (by a powerful political family) is evidence of the approach having had some sort of positive significance for 15th-century Italian society. The source is interpreted with confidence, related to its historical context, and shows an understanding of the need to interpret sources in the context of the society from which it is drawn – though not always too successfully.

Moderators' notes

Both responses attempt to analyse, understand and explain the significance of the pictorial sources with which they are working. Student 6 needs to pay much greater attention to the nature, origin and purpose of the cartoon.

Student 7 interrogates the evidence and begins to show how the evidence can be used to investigate the enquiry. For a mark in the higher level, Student 7 would need to develop more the relationship between the source and the issues it raises.

☞ Continued on the next two pages

Using artefacts and archaeological finds

Look at the ways in which these students have tackled the use of artefacts and archaeological finds as evidence in their enquiries.

Student 8: level 3 response

The student is here commenting on the Cuerdale Hoard, shown on the left, a treasure trove of Viking silver found in the banks of the river Ribble, near Preston, Lancashire in 1840.

> **'What was the short-term impact of Viking conquest and settlement in the years 890–910?'**

The Cuerdale Hoard was the most fantastic hoard of Viking silver ever to be found outside Russia. But what was it doing, buried in the bank of a river in Lancashire, and what can it tell us about Viking activity at that time?

The hoard consisted mainly of coins, ingots and jewellery. Altogether it weighed about 40 kg and was buried in a lead chest. It does not seem as if the silver had just been lost: it was buried there to keep it safe. It is significant that, in 902, the Vikings had been expelled from Dublin and the dates of the coins in the hoard suggest that it had been buried shortly afterwards.

A large number of the coins were minted in the Viking city of York and most of the bullion was of Irish–Norse origin. This suggests that the Ribble valley was an important route between York and the Irish Sea. It is thus very likely that the Hoard, hidden sometime after 910, was a sort of war chest, put together for an assault on Dublin in order to regain it. There were, too, local coins from Viking Northumbria, which further reinforces the idea that the Hoard was buried only a few years after the coinage was introduced.

In the Hoard there were arm rings and neck rings from Scandinavia, a Carolingian buckle, Permian rings, Slav beads and a Pictish comb. The coins came from England, (official Anglo-Saxon issues and coins from the Dane law) Frankish and Scandinavian coins as well as coins from the Islamic world. All of these are clearly indicative of Viking activities far away from their homelands. The far-flung places from which the silver came indicates either that the Vikings plundered wherever they went – and they went a long way – or that they traded far and wide.

The Cuerdale Hoard

This is a level 3 response. The student has placed the Cuerdale Hoard into its historical context, and using logic and cross-referencing to their own knowledge, has suggested a reason why it might have been hidden where it was. The contents of the Hoard have been interrogated with the view of finding out what light they shed on Viking activities at this time. This could have been developed further and related more closely to Viking activities in Western Europe.

As with written and pictorial sources, artefacts and archaeological finds need to be interrogated and then woven into the enquiry. Handled sensitively, they help clarify issues raised by the enquiry, support opinions and help shape your argument.

Pilgrimage of Grace badge

Student 9: level 4 response

The student is here commenting on a badge worn by one of the participants in the Pilgrimage of Grace, shown on the right. It is one of the sources used in the student's enquiry.

> **'What was the short-term significance of the Pilgrimage of Grace of 1536?'**
>
> The Pilgrimage of Grace was significant at the time because of the variety of concerns and motivations involved, and because of the way in which these combined to pose a threat to Henry VIII and his government. Although its name would suggest it was solely a religious uprising, this was not necessarily the case.
>
> The badge worn by Thomas Constable was beautifully embroidered and explicitly religious. It depicts the five wounds of Christ: his hands and feet, pierced by nails, are in the corners while the fifth wound is represented by the bleeding heart embroidered in the middle. This symbolism is heavily Catholic: the heart is shown as a wafer held over the chalice, which happened during the mass. In this way the rebellion can be seen as a protest against the dissolution of the monasteries and a desire to return to the 'olden days' of Catholicism.
>
> The very fact that those who joined in the Pilgrimage of Grace, and so became pilgrims, wore badges heavy with religious symbolism means that they were confident in their demands and, in the days before mass media, wanted them to be seem by the general populace who would understand their significance. This wasn't a hidden conspiracy but an open rebellion. The badges, too, served to bond the pilgrims and provide instant recognition of one another.
>
> The symbolism of the Five Wounds of Christ was replicated on the banners the pilgrims carried. Interestingly, the banner, produced by the rebels in the Lincolnshire town of Horncastle showed the Five Wounds but also added a plough and a horn, showing the rebels' additional concern about the impact of enclosure and the issue of a rumoured tax on horned cattle. Rumours like these fuelled the rebellion, creating a dangerous atmosphere of fear and tension. As the rebellion was not grounded in a single issue, it was more difficult for Henry to suppress and he could not meet all the demands.
>
> From analysing the badge it is clear that of itself it was a direct threat to Henry VIII and he and his supporters saw it as such.

This is a level 4 response. The student interrogates the source confidently in order to find out what it can provide as evidence relating to the short-term significance of the Pilgrimage of Grace. The student clearly relates this evidence to the Catholicism of England pre-dissolution and so to the importance of the Pilgrimage in challenging Henry VIII and his government. By regarding the badge as part of a wider identification of pilgrims, as evidenced by their banners, the student is identifying Thomas Constable's badge as being part of the whole and contributing to it. The source is contextualised well, and evaluated in the context of the values and assumptions of the society to which it belongs.

Weighing the evidence and reaching judgements

When you make a judgement about the short-term significance of the event, individual or factor you are investigating, you will need to weigh the evidence before you:

- To which sources will you give more weight?

- Whose evidence will you decide is the more credible?

- How will you reach your final conclusion?

This is how Student 10 tackled weighing up the evidence derived from an interrogation of sources used to research the Part A enquiry 'Assess the short-term significance of the 1918 Representation of the People Act in changing the status of women.'

The contemporary sources used in Student 10's response and evaluated were:

[1] Cartoon published in the magazine *Punch* 1918

[2] Unpublished letter from Agnes Woolfe to her mother, dated 31 August 1922

[3] Ray Strachey, *The Cause: a Short History of the Women's Movement in Britain*, published 1928

[4] An article 'The Equal Franchise' by Eva Hubback published in the journal *Fortnightly Review* in April 1928

[5] Christabel Pankhurst, *Unshackled: the Story of How We Won the Vote*, published 1959.

These sources have not been reproduced here. It is the way in which Student 10 weighs them up in the extract that is important.

In reaching a conclusion about the short-term significance of the 1918 Representation of the People Act in changing the status of women, it is necessary to decide what weight should be given to the evidence that has been derived from the source material. Should, for example, more weight be given to Christabel Pankhurst's book because she was involved in the suffragette movement, or to a private letter that was never intended to be published and so gives us an unbiased view? What weight should be given to a cartoon that was expressing the views of a magazine and was maybe simply capturing the enthusiasm of the moment? In reviewing the sources evaluated in this enquiry, it would seem sensible to place greatest weight on the evidence from Ray Strachey. Although she was herself involved in the suffrage movement, she wasn't interested in self-publicity to the extent that the Pankhursts were. The very title of Pankhurst's book gives a good clue as to its biased nature! Furthermore, Strachey's argument, as has been discussed already, is backed by Agnes's letter to her mother. Weight must be given, too, to Hubback's article, coming as it does just before the 1928 Act. We must, though, remember here that she and Strachey are looking at the significance of the Act from slightly different perspectives: Strachey and Woolfe at the immediate impact and Hubback from a nine- to ten-year perspective. In many ways they complement each other and together enable a judgement to be made.

The student is here standing back from the enquiry researched and the contemporary sources evaluated. The whole response, and the part played in it by the sources, is being reviewed and summarised in order to enable the student to reach a balanced judgement. The weight that should be placed on the evidence that has been derived from an evaluation of the contemporary sources is carefully considered and a conclusion reached based on this.

Reaching a supported judgement

Finally, you will need to reach an overall judgement about the significance of your event, individual or factor. Below is an example from a Part A enquiry in which Student 11 evaluated an individual's relevant strengths and weaknesses in order to come to a supported judgement. Here the student explains how a conclusion is being reached about the role of President Polk in the context of the Mexican–American War of 1846–8.

> **'Assess the short-term significance of the Mexican–American War of 1846–8.'**
>
> Throughout the Mexican campaign, Polk made many references to 'manifest destiny' and historians like Norton believe it was 'Polk's determination to fulfil the nation's manifest destiny to rule the continent' [1] that led to his decision to go to war. This is apparent in the President's message to Congress days before declaring war: 'we are called upon by every consideration of duty and patriotism to vindicate with decision the honor, the rights, and the interests of our country.' [2] Here he expresses his agenda in going to war and, although it is likely to be exaggerated in order to convince Congress to allow the war, Polk is a key figure in America, winning the majority vote and thus a figure of admiration for millions. Despite the validity of Polk's claims being debatable, his influence was not, and the view he held throughout the Mexican campaign that the conflict would bring 'vast benefits to the United States, to the commercial world and to the general interests of mankind' [3] is likely to have become a view held by many. It reached such an extent that, following the war, 'some rabid expansionists denounced the Treaty because it failed to include all of Mexico' [4] showing the vast differences between those who strongly opposed the war and those who yearned for as much expansion as possible. It could be suggested, therefore, that although Polk's attitude towards the war was considered 'a convenient rationalism for the conquest of lesser breeds like Mexicans', [5] it created a population of eager expansionists that can be seen throughout American history pushing for further expansion.

This is a level 4 response insofar as a supported judgement is concerned, marked according to the AO2 mark scheme (see pages 122–7) However it must be noted that this extract was selected because of the way in which the student supports the judgement about the role of President Polk. The student is not here weighing the status of the evidence.

The student is working with three contemporary sources and two secondary ones to reach a supported judgement about the role of President Polk in the Mexican–American War 1846–8. Knowledge about Polk's belief in 'manifest destiny' is supported by reference to historian Mary Norton and cross-referenced to Polk's speech of 11 May 1846, which is evaluated, and further cross-referenced to his speech a couple of years later. The response ends with a consideration of the treaty that ended the war with a reference to historian Paul Boyer and the judgement about Polk's attitude is therefore well-supported.

Essential notes

The Mexican–American War (1846–8) broke out after the US had annexed Texas in 1845. Mexico believed Texas belonged to them, despite the Texan Revolution (1836) against their rule. The war ended with the US acquiring the northern half of what was then Mexico, and which eventually became the states of California, Nevada, Arizona, New Mexico and Utah.

The numbers in the extract correspond to the following sources:

[1] Mary Norton, *A People and a Nation, Volume 1*, published 2006

[2] James K Polk May 11 1846

[3] President Polk from James Richardson, *Messages and Papers of the Presidents*, July 6 1848

[4] Paul Boyer, *The Enduring Vision*, published 2007

[5] Maldwyn Jones, *The limits of liberty: American history 1607–1992*, published 1995.

Moderators' notes

When it comes to writing up your enquiry you must remember to:

- select a range of sources that will develop the issues of the enquiry
- integrate their evidence into a structured and sustained argument.

Do
✓ Do use secondary sources to support or challenge your judgements about the evidence you have derived from evaluating contemporary sources.
✓ Do use secondary sources to develop and raise issues. Secondary sources are an excellent way to highlight and investigate themes, idea and opinions.

Do not
✗ Do not evaluate secondary sources. You won't get any marks for doing this. It will waste your time and take up words needed for explanation, evaluation of and analysis of contemporary sources and the issues they raise.
✗ Do not let references to secondary sources dominate your answer. Doing so wastes valuable word space and does not show your own thinking.

Using secondary sources

In researching for your Part A enquiry you will be using secondary sources to:

- explore the background to the topic you have chosen
- discover the issues that are relevant
- put the contemporary sources you are evaluating into their correct historical context.

These pages examine how to use secondary sources when writing up your Part A enquiry. Consider the examples below of the ways three students have used secondary sources in support of – or to challenge – evidence derived from contemporary sources.

Secondary sources: simple cross-referencing

'What was the short-term significance of Richard I in the Third Crusade?'

Richard's arrival in June 1191 changed everything. Beha ad-Din wrote 'The news of his coming had a dread and frightening effect on the hearts of Muslims.' At the battle of Ascalon he charged the Muslims with just ten knights until the rest of his men disembarked the ships. Jonathan Phillips agrees with Beha ad-Din when he writes of Richard's actions at the siege of Acre. He argues it was Richard's arrival that inspired the Franks to take the city. 'Phillip's presence had done little to hasten the fall of the city, but Richard's wealth, numerous siege engines and his personal vigour soon had an effect.'

The student is making a straightforward cross-reference between a modern historian's view of the impact of Richard I's arrival at Acre (Jonathan Phillips, *The Crusades 1095–1197*, published by Pearson 2002) and that of a contemporary Muslim writer. It is indicative of the qualities expected in a low level 3 response, marked using the AO1 mark scheme (see pages 122–3).

Secondary sources: cross-referencing for challenge

'Assess the short-term significance of Brigham Young.'

[The student considers some contemporary views of Brigham Young's leadership, and continues:]

Elements of suspicion and dictatorship are evident within his leadership. Noy suggests the existence of a secret group of Mormon operatives known as the 'Danites' or 'Destroying Angels' allegedly used to intimidate or silence opposition. Brogan, too, supports this notion of a secret police 'The Sons of Dan' and Young's personal militia 'The Nauvoo Legion'. Despite Young's refusal to acknowledge the existence of any such organisations in the interview conducted by Horace Greeley in 1859 ('HG: What do you say of the so-called Danites, or

Destroying Angels belonging to your church? BY: What do you say? I know of no such band, no such persons or organisation. I hear of them only in the slanders of our enemies.') the suspected presence of such secret groups suggests that Young himself was doubtful of his own authority and suspicious of, and even paranoid about, opposition.

The student is using two modern historians to challenge Brigham Young's assertion that he knew of no secret police operating in Salt Lake City. In doing so, issues about the nature of Brigham Young's leadership are being raised. This is indicative of work at high level 3, marked according to the AO1 mark scheme (see pages 122–3).

Secondary sources: cross-referencing for support and challenge

'Assess the short-term significance of Deng Xiaoping, 1978–98.'

[The student provides evidence from a range of sources about the impact Deng had on the Chinese economy and continues:]

Brown states that 'China started to commit something like 45% of its annual GDP to investment in railways, buildings and infrastructure' confirming the views of *Time* magazine that China was 'exceeding its ambitious target of an annual 7% growth rate'. However, there is an argument that there are some negative aspects of the economic development of China, more so in the 1990s. Predominantly it is the secondary sources that focus mainly on the economic successes of the Deng era, whereas the contemporary sources seem, with the support of only some secondary sources, to take a different view and focus on the negative aspects. The New York Times, for example, found that little was being done to bring 'corruption under control'. This is supported by Stephen, who recognises that 'corruption remains chronic and contagious.' That corruption was an underlying factor during Deng's economic reforms would seem to negate the economic significance of his era because so much more could have been done.

The student is using the work of modern historians (Kerry Brown, *Friends and Enemies: the Past, Present and Future of the Communist Party of China,* published by Anthem Press 2009) to support and to challenge the views expressed in the journal *Time* and the newspaper *The New York Times*. This is indicative of work at level 4, marked according to the AO1 mark scheme (see pages 122–3).

Moderators' notes

Remember that secondary sources have a strictly limited role in your Part A enquiry. They support or challenge your judgements, and help develop your ideas around issues. Do not, whatever you do, evaluate them!

Moderators' notes

Students working on 20th- and 21st-century topics should use historians as secondary sources and other commentaries as contemporary sources.

Using secondary source material

You will be doing a lot of wider reading and note-taking in connection with your Part B enquiry. It is important that you tease out the different kinds of reading you will be doing. Pages 56–63 outline how you will be reading for information, reading for opinion and argument, and reading to raise issues.

The difficulty here is in the texts. Historians rarely separate a particular topic into neat, easy-to-handle sections. The information, opinion, argument and issues are naturally mixed up in the process of writing good history. Moreover, historians do not always make clear when they are giving their own opinion, the opinion of others, or just the facts. You need to be alert!

Close reading of this kind means you need to approach the text methodically:

1. Read through – or scan – the text. This will give you a working understanding of the 'story'.

2. Read carefully through the text a second time; only now make a note of the factual information. If the historian expresses doubt or seems unsure about a fact, then make sure you are critical in your reading of it.

3. Jot down any opinions expressed personally by the historian. These opinions help shape the historian's overall view.

4. Finally, use the opinions to write down what you think the historian is trying to say. Doing so helps shine a light on the issues. It also helps define the historian's argument.

Consider the examples that follow on close reading of secondary source texts.

Reading for information

Read the paragraph below. The author is writing about Henry V's premature death, leaving behind an eight-month-old son and heir.

Secondary Source 1
(From Juliet Barker, *Conquest: The English Kingdom of France 1417–1450*, published by Little, Brown 2009)

The prospects were certainly not good: **assuming he lived to come of age, Henry VI's minority would be the longest in England's history.** To compound the problem, there were **two kingdoms to rule, each with its own institutions, laws, customs and personnel.** Quite how this was to be done became a matter of fevered debate in both countries. **In England, Gloucester tried to assert his right to be regent on the grounds that his brother had appointed him to the 'chief guardianship and wardship' of Henry VI. Parliament would have none of it: the codicil referred only to the young king's person, not to the realm, and in any case the late king had no power to alter precedent and law without the assent of parliament. Constitutionally, the right to govern England should fall to Gloucester's elder brother, who was next in line to the succession,** but **Bedford was still in France** and likely to remain there. A compromise was therefore reached. **On 5 December 1422 Bedford was appointed protector, defender and chief councillor of England, but would only exercise these powers when he was in the country: in his absence they would be held by Gloucester. The arrangement ensured the separation of crowns envisaged by the Treaty of Troyes and prevented Bedford from ruling England from France.**

The factual information contained in this paragraph is in bold, and there is certainly a lot here. The historian, Juliet Gardner, is describing the situation regarding the governance of England, and England's possessions in France, at the beginning of the minority of Henry VI. She hardly gives her own opinion – 'prospects were not good' and 'fevered debate' – and uses the final sentence to pull all the information together by explaining the significance of the division of work between the Dukes of Gloucester and Bedford.

In terms of what to use in support of your Part B enquiry, this text is excellent for knowing what went on. It is an information text. If you were going to use it as a basis for your argument, you would have to supplement it with your own strongly supported opinions.

Now read the following secondary source:

> **Secondary Source 2**
> (From G. R. Elton, *England under the Tudors*, published by Methuen 1955)
>
> Wolsey turned out to be the most disappointing man who ever held great power in England and used it for so long with skill and high intelligence. **He survived for a year after his fall.** Saved from imprisonment by Henry's unwonted mercy, **restored to part of his preferments and property**, he determined to devote himself to his **archbishopric of York**, which he had never yet visited. But the pull of the great world proved too strong. **He moved north slowly**, casting longing glances over his shoulder; he continued to excite hostile comment by his lavish living; finally **he involved himself in plots which his enemies turned against him. In November 1530 the council had him arrested and conveyed to London;** he knew what was in store. **By easy stages the ailing man reached Leicester; there, met by the captain of the king's guard, he died on 24th.**

The factual information in this paragraph is in bold. Note how little there is. Geoffrey Elton is here painting more of a pen picture of the last days of Cardinal Wolsey. He is skilfully building up an image of the man whilst combining it with information. Elton couldn't possibly know, for example, that Wolsey was determined to devote himself to his bishopric of York, that the pull of the world proved too strong and that he knew what was in store for him on his return to London. Elton is here making intelligent guesses, based on his knowledge and understanding of the situation at the time – but this is not factual information. Note, too, that Elton begins this paragraph by giving us his own opinion about Wolsey: that he was the 'most disappointing man who ever held great power in England'. This all makes for lively and interesting reading, and exactly the sort of material you would want if you were going to tease out the views and attitudes of historians, but not too heavy on information.

So, in terms of reading for information, the first extract is clearly of more use. However, if you are looking for opinion, and if you need ideas, then the second extract provides a good basis for an enquiry into Henry VIII and the exercise of power.

Essential notes

The Treaty of Troyes (May 1420) was an agreement that Henry V of England and his heirs would inherit the throne of France on the death of Charles VI of France. The treaty preserved the laws and government of each kingdom.

Essential notes

Cardinal Wolsey (1473–1530) was a cardinal of the Catholic Church and Lord Chancellor (1515–29) in Henry VIII's government. He fell largely because he failed to get the Pope to agree to a divorce between Henry VIII and Catherine of Aragon.

☞ **Continued on the six pages**

Reading for opinion and argument

As seen in secondary Source 2 (see page 57) some historians manage to weave their own views and attitudes into their writing. It wouldn't be too difficult to work out that G. R. Elton was not a great supporter of Wolsey – at least, not in that paragraph. Historians interpret the facts, form opinions and make a case for what they believe. Here, Elton's opinion of Wolsey's character is not high, and through this he is possibly building a case for the Cardinal being the architect of his own downfall.

Other historians are even more obvious in stating their opinions. Look, for example, at the following secondary source:

What case is Corrigan making? Well, clearly, the first clue lies in the title, and the use of the words 'arrogance' and 'myths'. Overall, he is saying that there was no substance whatsoever to Operation Sea Lion because Germany did not have the ability to mount a sustained invasion of Britain. He is also pouring scorn on the ability of the Home Guard to defend the country, and maintaining that the Royal Navy would sacrifice the Home Fleet in order to defeat any potential sea-borne invasion by the Germans. In doing so, he is adding another important piece to his argument with regards to the brutal reality of war, decision-making and the myths perpetuated by Churchill, the wartime propaganda machine and subsequent Churchill-friendly histories vis-à-vis the possibility of invasion.

Essential notes

The Home Guard was an organisation established in 1940. It was a branch of the British Army, and was intended to be a defence force in case of an invasion by Nazi Germany. The Home Guard patrolled Britain's shores and guarded key places such as factories and railway stations. It consisted of volunteers who, for a variety of reasons, were not eligible for military service. The Home Guard was disbanded in December 1945.

Essential notes

Operation Sea Lion (Unternehmen Seelowe) was Germany's plan to invade Britain in 1940.

In your own reading about the topic you are researching, you will find writing as incisive and as outspoken as this. Do not dismiss it. It may be the result of great research. It may represent a breakthrough in the way we look at an event, historical figure and associated factors and patterns of change. If you disagree, then it is important that you find evidence to contradict the argument. If you agree, then, by the same token, it is important that you use other secondary evidence to back up the argument. Either way, use it in your enquiry to show that you have read widely and can evaluate arguments.

Naturally, opinionated history writing is the result of debate. Historians will interpret facts in different ways. They will disagree with each other. Through the force of argument, they try to persuade you to believe in their take on a given subject.

Read, for example, the following two secondary sources, each of which is making a case for their views on the standard of living during the Industrial Revolution:

Secondary Source 4
(From E. P. Thompson, *The Making of the English Working Class,* published by Pantheon 1963)

In the first fifty years of the Industrial Revolution the working class share of the national product had almost certainly fallen relative to the share of the property-owning and professional classes. The 'average' working man remained very close to subsistence level at a time when he was surrounded by the evidence of the increase of national wealth, much of it obviously the product of his own labour, passing equally obviously into the hands of his employers. In psychological terms, this felt very much like a decline in standards.

Secondary Source 5
(From M. Hartwell, 'The Standard of Living Debate,' published by Wiley in the *Economic History Review*, 1963)

The standard of living controversy has been confused about values and by people talking about different things. I have argued that the standard of living of the mass of people of England was improving, slowly during the French Wars (1793–1815), more quickly after 1815. Increasing real income is no measure of people's ultimate well-being and the period of the Industrial Revolution was one of political discontent and social upheaval. But, in terms of the large number of jobs created and the mobility of labour, it was also a period of opportunity for working class men and women.

Essential notes

The Industrial Revolution was a period from roughly 1750 to about 1880. It started with the mechanisation of the textile industry, which meant that it moved from being a domestic-based industry to one centred on factories. This in turn impacted on the coal, iron and steel industries, and led to an increase in the demand for goods. This demand was met by the introduction of canals, improved roads and, eventually, railways. The impact on the people was enormous, as thousands of people moved from the countryside into the expanding industrial towns.

Continued on the next four pages

These are two very different views on the same subject. Again, do not dismiss one or the other. If your enquiry is on exactly this subject, then these two perspectives could form the basis of your own argument. Or, you may want to examine each in order to advance a third argument. If, in your reading, you find historians disagreeing about an event, person, factor or theme, you need to note this. Note not just that they disagree, but also on which aspects they disagree:

- Are they the same?

- Are they using different evidence to reach these conflicting conclusions?

Note, also, that both extracts were written in the same year. From this, you can surmise that both historians will have had access to almost exactly the same information, and that they might have read all the same secondary accounts of the period.

Clearly, the examples show that well-researched, strongly expressed opinions in secondary sources are extremely useful when it comes to writing up your own enquiry. It is important that you make use of the issues raised and show – by comparing two or more different secondary sources – that you are aware of the thinking around your particular topic, and that you are able to use the secondary sources to get as close to the truth as possible.

Considering all the secondary sources

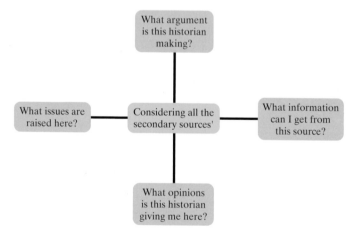

Reading to raise issues

In all your reading around the topic you are studying for your Part B enquiry, there will be indications as to issues you may wish to pursue. Look, for example, at the issues raised by Secondary Sources 1–5.

Secondary sources used:

1. From Juliet Barker, *Conquest: The English Kingdom of France 1417–1450*, published by Little, Brown 2009

2. From G. R. Elton, *England under the Tudors*, published by Methuen 1955

3. From C. Corrigan, *Blood, Sweat and Arrogance and the Myths of Churchill's War*, published by Weidenfeld & Nicolson 2006

4. From E. P. Thompson, *The Making of the English Working Class*, published by Pantheon 1963

5. From M. Hartwell, 'The Standard of Living Debate' published by Wiley in the *Economic History Review*, 1963

Secondary Sources	Issues
Secondary Source 1	Did the division of power and responsibility between Bedford and Gloucester work out in reality?
Secondary Source 2	To what extent was Wolsey the architect of his own downfall?
Secondary Source 3	How realistic was Operation Sea Lion?
Secondary Source 4	Was the apparent fall in the standard living psychological or supporte by data?
Secondary Source 5	What data is being used by those engaged in the standard of living controversy?

The raising of issues through your reading of secondary sources provides the key(s) to the quality of your own enquiry. When reading, therefore, it is important that you make use of both the factual information and the variety of opinions to extract the main issues surrounding your topic. When you come across an issue, make sure you:

- make a note of it

- express it in a question

- compare and contrast it to other same-topic issues

- consider how the issue relates to your main line of enquiry.

Continued on the next two pages

Essential notes

The English Civil War (1642–51) was a series of battles between Parliamentarians and Royalists. It ended with the victory of the Parliamentarians at Worcester in September 1651.

Oliver Cromwell (1599–1658) was one of the commanders of the New Model Amy that defeated the Royalists in the English Civil War. Following the beheading of King Charles I, England became a republic with Cromwell as Lord Protector.

Read the following two examples in terms of issues raised.

Secondary Source 6

(From Barry Coward, *Oliver Cromwell*, published by Longman 1991)

The Civil War shaped Oliver Cromwell's political outlook in two major ways. First, it confirmed the belief he had already adopted by 1642: that the war was a just one and that he and the king's opponents had God's support. Even though, as will be seen, his military career before the battle of Marston Moor on 2 July 1644 does not merit the excessive praise it has often been given, Cromwell did help to prevent eastern England from falling wholly into Royalist hands. He interpreted this limited success as clear evidence of God's blessing. Moreover, especially after the battle of Marston Moor, his self-confidence increased to such an extent that first others, and then Cromwell himself, came to believe that he and the army had a divinely ordained mission to win the war and bring about a godly reformation.

The second effect of the Civil War on Cromwell was to shatter his political innocence. As the war developed he realised that not all his wartime allies shared either his desire to prosecute the war wholeheartedly or his hopes that the outcome of the king's defeat would be godly reformation. Increasingly he found himself at odds, not only with Royalist troops, but with 'enemies within' the parliamentary alliance. The sense of shock and disillusionment he felt at this discovery forced him to abandon his naïve belief that all he needed to do was to prosecute the war effectively in defence of parliamentary liberties. Instead, he came to see that, if the war was to result in a godly reformation, it would have to be fought in the political arena as well as on the battlefield.

Issues raised by Secondary Source 6

Points of issue	Issues expressed as a question
Cromwell's belief in divine right	In what way did civil war reinforce Cromwell's belief that the war was sanctioned by a Protestant God?
Cromwell's politicisation	How did Cromwell come to realise that the alliance was driven by personal interests?

In terms of making use of the issues raised, the student would then need to consider their own line of enquiry. A decision with regard to the importance of each issue would then be made, and so the student would be able to either include or discard one or both of the issues.

Secondary Source 7
(From R. Evans, *The Third Reich in Power*, published by Penguin 2005)

The problem with arguing about whether or not the Third Reich modernised German society, how far it wanted to change the social order and in what ways it succeeded in doing so, is that society was not really a priority of Nazi policy anyway. True, social divisions were to be, if not abolished altogether, then at least bridged over, social discord was to be replaced by social harmony, and status, though not class, was to be equalised as far as possible in new Reich. But much of this was to be achieved by symbols, rituals and rhetoric. Above all, what Hitler and the Nazis wanted was a change in people's spirit, their way of thinking and their way of behaving. They wanted a new man, and for that matter, a new woman, to emerge out of the ashes of the Weimar Republic, re-creating the fighting unity and commitment of the Front in the First World War. Their revolution was first and foremost cultural rather than social. Yet it was underpinned by something more concrete, that had real physical consequences for thousands, and in the end millions of Germans, Jews and others: the idea of racial engineering, of scientifically moulding the German people into a new breed of heroes, and its corollary, of eliminating the weak from the chain of heredity and taking those who were seen as Germany's enemies, real and potential, out of the re-forged national community altogether.

Essential notes

The Weimar Republic was the parliamentary republic established in Germany in 1919 after the end of the First World War. The Third Reich was the name given to the state set up by the Nazis in 1933 once Hitler became Chancellor of Germany.

Issues raised by Secondary Source 7

Points of issue	Issues expressed as a question
Change in society not a Nazi priority	Was Hitler concerned with actually changing the structure of post-WW1 German society?
Nazi priority was creation of a new German, irrespective of position Cultural revolution	What was the Nazi programme with regards to German society?
New German defined by what it was not – Jewish, other, non-Aryan, etc.	What was the point of Germany's philosophy of racial engineering?

Clearly, the above issues are related, and you may be inclined to think of merging at least one with another. Whatever you do, do not discard any of them before relating them to your enquiry.

As you read to raise issues, you will be looking for ideas and for points of analysis made by historians that you may want to take further. Historians' analyses may look impressive and interesting, but you do need to ask how appropriate and useful their analysis is to your own particular enquiry. Use tables as shown above as a means of noting issues raised in your own reading, and then expressing them as questions. This way, you will be able to relate them to the main thrust of your enquiry and so decide as to their relevance.

Essential notes

You could keep your resource record electronically, as a blog. Talk to your teachers about this, because they will have to be sure it is workable in your school situation.

Using the resource record

It is really important that you complete your resource record as you research your Part A and Part B enquiries. There are two main reasons for this:

1. So that your teachers and the examination board know that the research is your own.

2. So that your teachers can help guide your research.

How the resource record works

Every time you use a particular resource, note it down, add an appropriate comment, and date the entry.

Your teacher will look at your resource record at regular intervals, putting a date and their initials when they do so, and adding a comment if it is appropriate for them to do so. In this way your teacher can monitor what you are doing, and know that you are doing the research yourself.

You and your teacher will talk about your research at regular intervals. Part of this conversation will involve going through your research record with you. It is here that your teacher can, for example, suggest other sources you might consult and will be able to make sure that your research is keeping on track.

Using the resource record with a Part A enquiry

The following is an example of how one student started a resource record for a Part A enquiry.

The Part A enquiry was looking at the significance of the contribution Malcolm X made to the civil rights movement in the USA:

- This student has clearly identified the issues considered relevant to the enquiry.

- The student has found some useful contemporary sources that would hopefully enable the issues to be developed.

- The student's comments are clear. If the student goes on to select more contemporary sources than needed, it will be easy to go back and sort out which are best at addressing the different focuses of the enquiry.

- The teacher has been encouraging and helpful, and has made some comments that are challenging the student to think about how the sources will be used.

- The student and the teacher have dated entries, and this helped the moderator to see that the student really has done the work.

Essential notes

Malcolm X was an African-American Muslim minister who was active in promoting civil rights for African-Americans. As one of the leaders of the Nation of Islam he advocated black supremacy and the separation of black and white Americans. This was in contrast to the civil rights movement that focused on integration. After leaving the Nation of Islam in 1964, he moved closer to the main US civil rights movement. Members of the Nation of Islam assassinated him in 1965 when he was 39 years old.

Issue	Source	Comments	Teacher's comments
Malcolm X's political and ideological views	*The Autobiography of Malcolm X* by Malcolm X and Alex Haley, 1965 Contemporary	I found this source to be very helpful in terms of analysing Malcolm X as a person, instead of just his political views. However, it did allow me to truly understand his political and ideological views, which I could therefore apply to my work via facts and quotes, which through the book I had an understanding about, this therefore allowed me to integrate it into my work in a manner effective of answering my question. (27.9.2010)	You clearly understand the importance of this material and how to apply it. JB (8.10.2010)
Malcolm X change of focus	Malcolm X, The Ballot or the Bullet Speech, 3 April 1964 Contemporary	I found this particular source to be effective in pinpointing the change in Malcolm's views, which in relation to my question was incredibly important as it spawned some of his greatest contributions to the civil rights movement and therefore played an important role in my coursework (4.10. 2010)	Good to consider change in perspective over time. How are you going to use this to focus on short-term significance? JB (21.10.10)
What drove him?	Malcolm X, the *Playboy* Interview, May 1963 Contemporary	I was able to use this source in a manner that again allowed me to compare Malcolm's views and how they changed the contribution he put into the civil rights movement. In an analytical context it allowed me to express Malcolm's passion, which drove his significance in the movement. (16.10.2010)	Aim to use sources to develop the argument. Can this be used to support or challenge others? JB (21.10.2010)
Broadening range of appeal	Malcolm X 12 Dec 1964, New York City Contemporary	This particular source helped me outline and emphasise how Malcolm had come to significantly contribute towards the brotherhood of all men and not black supremacy. Overall, this source helped me to understand how Malcolm's contribution changed but didn't lose its significance. (25.11.2010)	Good, again addressing change over time and subsequent impact. JB (16.12.2010)
Significance?	Malcolm X 31 December 1964 (taken from the essay 'Malcolm X our revolutionary son and brother' by Patricia Robinson Secondary	By using this source I was able to show how Malcolm contributed not only to the present generation, but the upcoming one. Overall a helpful source in showing Malcolm's significance. (5.12.2010)	Good comment relating to significance. BUT now review your sources to see if you have sufficient range. Remember to use this source in support or challenge of judgements reached by your evaluation of contemporary sources JB (16.12.2010)

Continued on the next two pages

Moderators' notes

The resource record here and on page 64 are not the complete records, but show clearly and well how they should be filled in.

Essential notes

Cardinal Richelieu was King Louis XIII's chief minister 1624–42. He aimed to consolidate royal power and crush domestic factions by reducing the power of the nobility. He succeeded in transforming France into a strong, centralised state.

Using the resource record with a Part B enquiry

Consider the example below and table opposite, and how one student started a resource record for a Part B enquiry.

The Part B enquiry was looking into the role of individuals in strengthening the French monarchy 1589–1715:

- The student has here just begun reading in connection with the Part B enquiry.

- The student has started to identify relevant issues and the reading that will help develop these.

- The student has identified the strength of the secondary sources that have been accessed, and hasn't been afraid to say where it is a bit unclear as to how to use one of them.

- The teacher has made some helpful suggestions regarding using Richelieu's words as a useful starting point – and suggesting the need for cross-referencing.

- The teacher and student have dated their entries and in this way they can both keep track of the progress of the research.

Issue	Source	Comments	Teacher's comments
Nature of the French monarchy	Alan James, *The Origins of French Absolutism 1598–1661* pub Pearson Longman 2006	Useful because of my enquiry focus; provides necessary detail and an indication as to issues I should follow. (10.01.2011)	Good. Use this in planning your approach and for rising issues, but remember to keep focused on strengthening the French monarchy. HS (20.1.11)
Richelieu and foreign policy	Pierre Grillon (ed), *Les Papiers de Richelieu* Vol 1 pub Editions A Pedone 1977	I could use this to relate to the needs of France or the needs of the French monarchy; am unclear as to how to use it to show how Richelieu strengthened the French monarchy – or weakened it. (25.1.2011)	Perhaps check again as you have Richelieu's own words here. This could be a useful starting point for looking at his impact on the monarchy. HS (30.1.2011)
Role played by Henri IV	www.le.ac.uk	Concise overview of Henri IV's methods to stabilise France. Also good factual evidence. (28.1.2011)	Remember factual evidence can 'bump up' against other source material. Cross-referencing would be effective here. HS (30.1.2011)

The importance of using a resource record

You can see that a resource record is a really useful working document:

- it helps you to identify issues and related source material

- it enables you and your teacher to keep track of the progress of your research

- it has to be sent in to the moderator so that the moderator can see that you really have done the work yourself.

Moderators' notes

It is not necessary to use sources contemporary to the period in Part B, but you can consult them if they provide useful information.

Using a resource record

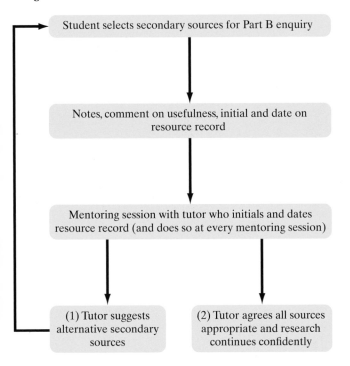

Moderators' notes

Discuss your resource record with your teacher so your research is clear and focused.

Planning the write-up of your Part A and Part B enquiries

Your complete assignment is made up of Part A and Part B. You may have been advised by your teacher to:

- write up the Part A enquiry first because it may be easier to focus on short-term outcomes

- write up the Part B enquiry first because you will probably have researched that immediately following the taught overview

- complete all the research on both your Part A and Part B enquiries, and then write them both up, one after the other.

Getting ready to plan

In order to plan effectively, you will need to have:

- identified issues and collated enquiry-relevant contemporary sources for use in Part A of your assignment

- identified issues and collated enquiry-relevant secondary sources for use in Part B of your assignment

- for Part A, collected and collated your notes on the secondary sources you used to provide contextual knowledge about the short-term significance of the individual, event, factor or movement you have chosen, and to support and challenge the judgements made from an evaluation of your contemporary sources

- for Part B, collected and collated your notes from your wider reading of secondary sources that discuss the process of change, and that provide evidence for a key factor or turning point

- considered and organised the relevant issues.

All the above information will be in your resource record and in your notes. You will have retained your reference lists, your collections of analysed sources and your collections of enquiry-related issues. Your notes will contain factual information, background reading and opinions and arguments related to particular issues. Your job now is to arrange these in a way that is manageable. This way, you gain an overview of your assignment before beginning.

Finally, you should be aware that your teacher can, at this point, give you no further advice or guidance.

The importance of planning

A well-thought out plan is the key to success. A plan enables you to:

- think through your ideas

- organise your ideas into a logical progression

- make sure you stay focused on the enquiry question

- decide where it is appropriate to introduce source evaluation (Part A) and evidence of wider reading (Part B)

- create and develop an argument

- reach well-supported judgements.

Moderators' notes

You must plan both your Part A and your Part B response. You will have done a lot of work on your coursework topic and probably have a very good idea of what the conclusions to your research will be. Do not be tempted to think that you know what you are going to say and start writing. It is very important at this stage that you do not rush. Plan carefully how you are going to present your findings and show how you have reached a supported judgement. Not to do so will result in work that isn't carefully thought through, is unbalanced and poorly argued. Your final mark (and grade) will then not be as high as it should be.

Your plan should contain:

- Lines, or strands, of your argument that focus on the issues you have identified.
- The key points you are going to put in each paragraph to show how your argument will be developed.
- Support for the argument you are presenting. This will come from source evaluation (Part A) and evidence of wide reading of secondary sources (Part B).

What your plan looks like depends very much on you. You will have worked with plans and writing frames in the past, and you will know which one suits you best.

Example writing frame

This is an example of one way to plan that could be used for a Part B enquiry:

Structure	Content
Introduction	Setting out the main issues
Paragraphs 1–3	Analysis of presented key factor or turning point
	Evidence of wider reading
Paragraph 4	Analysis of second alternative key factor or key turning point
	Evidence of wider reading
Paragraph 5	Analysis of third alternative key factor or key turning point
	Evidence of wider reading
Conclusion	A considered, supported judgement as to which is key

The importance of reviewing your plan

Once you have drawn up your plan, do not immediately start writing. Pause for a moment, stand back and review it.

Planning checklist

Have you …	Yes
Included everything you wanted to address?	
Presented it in a logical way?	
Made your line of argument clear?	
Supported your conclusions?	
Provided evidence of wide reading?	

If you are certain that you can answer 'Yes' to all five questions, you are ready to start writing up. When you have finished writing up each part of your assignment, return to this reviewing checklist to make sure you have done what you set out to do.

Moderators' notes

1. At least a third of your response should be dealing with an explanation and analysis of the given key factor or key turning point in the enquiry title.
2. You must cover the whole chronology of the coursework programme you have followed.
3. You do need to show evidence of wider reading. It may not be appropriate to do this in every paragraph; so much depends on the topic and the number of historians you have been able to access.
4. The teacher-moderator and the Edexcel moderator need to see your views and supported judgements too!

Essay writing skills for Parts A and B

These next pages will deal with essay writing skills: the introduction, the conclusion and creating a sustained argument. These skills relate to your whole assignment: to both Part A and to Part B.

Writing your introduction

When thinking about your introduction, remember to:

- set out the case you are going to make

- address the enquiry directly

- define any key terms.

Consider the focus and strengths of the following introductions and think about how you are going to construct your own introduction.

Example introduction for a Part A enquiry

Student 1

> **'What was the short-term significance of the Tiananmen Square massacre of 1989?'**
>
> The short-term significance of an event is best defined as the impact it had over a period spanning from immediately following the event up until twenty years later. It is undeniable that the Tiananmen Square massacre of 1989 was greatly significant. The event revealed divisions within the CCP with the resurgence of hardliners and Deng's political manoeuvring, as evidenced in a number of contemporary accounts, such as excerpts from a CCP meeting, and Kate Adie's documentary. This source also raises another important outcome of the event: the sacrifice of political freedom to safeguard the continuation of economic reform, which is supported by historians Fenby and Gittings. Whilst many sources support the view that China's economy boomed from the nineties onwards, others consider the economic impact caused by international condemnation of the massacre, which also strained China's foreign relations. Perhaps the most significant outcome of Tiananmen, however, was that it ended the democracy movement in China and therefore secured the continuation of the CCP's rule.

The introduction starts off by defining what the student means by 'short-term significance'. It then moves on to indicate the areas the student will be looking at and the type of contemporary sources that will be used. The introduction ends by giving a very strong indication as to what the student will find to have been the most significant outcome of the Tiananmen Square massacre. This is a very good, and clear, introduction to a Part A enquiry.

Essential notes

The Tiananmen Square massacre happened in the streets around Tiananmen Square, Beijng, on 4 June 1984 when the Chinese People's Liberation Army opened fire on mainly student protestors who were demonstrating against the slow speed of reform. The exact number of civilian deaths is not known: estimates range from hundreds to thousands. The massacre led to worldwide protests and western governments imposed economic sanctions on China. Inside China, the authorities arrested and imprisoned protestors and purged those they thought sympathetic to the protests.

Example introduction for a Part B enquiry
Student 2

> 'In considering the development of Renaissance thought and culture between 1350 and 1530, how far can the Medici coup be seen as a key turning point?'
>
> The Renaissance period spanning the years 1350–1530 marked a dramatic change in art, politics, literature and humanism throughout Florence and, later, Rome. This period saw the development of Petrarch's Christian humanism to civic humanism through individuals such as Bruni, Colucio and Niccoli. The Renaissance, meaning re-birth, witnessed the re-introduction of classical ideas in literature and politics, helped by Alberti and later Machiavelli, and also in art and architecture, as the 1400s saw a change from international gothic to classical realism. Much evidence suggests the turning point within the Renaissance was the Medici coup of 1434, due to the patronage and funding this family offered. Baron would argue that an important key event was the Florence-Milan war of 1400–02 because this introduced classical literature. Other historians, such as Stringer, would place Rome at the centre, with events such as the Papal return to Rome in 1447 playing a key role. However, it will be argued that these events were milestones compared to the impact on culture and the arts, which the Medici coup produced.

The introduction starts by outlining the main themes of the Renaissance, and the individuals involved. The student then turns to wider reading of secondary sources and the emphasis placed by some historians on alternative key turning points. The introduction ends by making a clear statement as to the position the student will take in their analysis of the potential turning points. This is an excellent introduction to a Part B enquiry.

Qualities of an effective introduction
The qualities of an effective introduction are shown in the examples above:

- each begins with a broad statement
- for Part A, Student 1 defines the terms of the enquiry
- for Part B, Student 2 sets the scene for the enquiry
- each follows up by addressing the subject of the enquiry, while at the same time listing the issues that will form the main part of the assignment
- each finishes by showing how the assignment will end.

Essential notes
The Medici family and their supporters gained control of the city of Florence in 1434, and kept control of the city until 1494. Cosimo de'Medici's patronage of the arts transformed Florence into the leading city of the Italian Renaissance.

Moderators' notes
Quality of written communication

Account will be taken of the way in which you communicate the findings of your two enquiries. You need to make sure that your work is grammatically correct and that your spelling is correct. You need to make sure, too, that your ideas are properly organised into separate paragraphs, and that your response starts with an introduction and ends with a conclusion.

If the historical understanding you are showing is much better than the ways in which you are expressing it, then you will be marked towards the bottom of the level into which your response falls.

Of the student assignments on pages 78–119, the Part B enquiry beginning on page 92 is an example of an enquiry where the quality of the history is much better than the quality of the ways in which it is expressed.

☞ Continued on the next two pages

How to create a coherent and sustained argument

Pages 68–9 outlined how important it is to plan your Part A and Part B enquiries that together will make up your whole assignment. One very important reason for doing this is that you need to create an argument that develops logically throughout the paragraphs you write. In this way you will create a coherent and sustained argument that will score highly.

There are three key things you need to do.

1. Argue: when planning, you will have decided on the lines of each argument you will be making. Separate them out, and begin a new line of argument with a new paragraph.

2. Explain: continue the paragraph by explaining your line of argument.

3. Support: always provide evidence to support your line of argument. If you do not do this, your argument will not be an argument but will become an assertion, and that will not gain you many marks.

Using and evaluating source materials for a Part A enquiry

In each paragraph, it is important that you recognise the difference between evaluating contemporary source materials and using secondary sources in support or challenge. Consider the following example from one student:

Student 3

'What was the short-term significance of Pearl Harbor for international relations in the years up to 1945?'

American entry into the war coincided with a flourish of nationalism and mobilisation of efforts towards the war, illustrated in a cartoon published by David Low in the *Evening Standard*. The cartoon shows a British and American officer, together saluting the Statue of Liberty. The words 'United one hundred per cent war basis' are included, suggesting the alliance was at its optimum strength and was fully orientated and focused for the war ahead with both countries 'one hundred per cent' geared for success. However, the positioning of both servicemen saluting the Statue of Liberty and not anything specifically British does imply the superiority of the USA in any alliance. The political stance of the *Evening Standard* does need to be considered. Traditionally right-wing, it could be attempting to appease its readers, with views of a nationalist nature. Potentially, it was in their interest to stir up support for the war and American intervention. It is true that the strength of both countries, taken together, did prove superior to Japan's, a view supported by historian A.J.P. Taylor who agrees that the allies' focus and superior capability proved decisive in the conflict.

The student here begins by interrogating a cartoon and drawing evidence from this. The student develops this by considering the intentions of the cartoonist and the underlying message of the cartoon as well as the more obvious message. The surface message of the cartoon is explained, that Britain and the USA will be standing shoulder to shoulder in the forthcoming conflict, but the student also points to the underlying message that Britain is the junior partner in this relationship. The student goes on to

Moderators' notes

It is important that you separate the points into paragraphs. Each paragraph should open with a phrase that encourages opinion. For example: *It could be argued that… On the other hand… It seems that… Without a doubt…*

Essential notes

In December of 1941, the Japanese airforce attacked the US fleet base at Pearl Harbor, in Hawaii. Previously remaining neutral, this attack brought the USA into the Second World War.

support this by referencing the view of historian A.J.P Taylor. But note that, whilst the contemporary source is evaluated, the secondary source is only used in support and is not evaluated. This is how it should be.

Showing evidence of wider reading and secondary sources in a Part B enquiry

When writing up your Part B enquiry, it is important that you show that you have read widely. Your analysis has to be supported by well-selected information, of course, but it needs to go further than that if you are aiming for high marks. You need to show that you have consulted a wide range of sources in following your enquiry. Consider the following example from one student:

Student 4

> **'Assess the significance of the influence of American ideology on the process of the settlement of the West between 1789 and 1906.'**
>
> Although not a solid, measurable entity, the phenomenon that is American ideology and expansionism is one debated much by historians, the idea that the pure drive and hunger to gain more land is enough to push a whole nation in movement from East to West, a factor without which the process may not have taken place so rapidly. It is a view strongly shared by historian Turner that 'American intellect will continually demand a wider field for its exercise' that 'restless, nervous energy, that dominant individualism' is enough to drive a man across a whole nation to satisfy his innate desire to strive for something further and better as soon as the opportunity presents itself. Not only Turner, but Norton believed 'since colonial days, Americans have hungered for land', suggesting the 'innate desire' that Turner speaks of has been present since 1783, and has just continued to grow over the century that followed. However, historians like Worster disagree. They have never been able to see the West as some sort of process in motion, maintaining that such a grand narrative of expansion couldn't be accounted for simply by a common ideology. Expansion, they maintain, has to be explained by a combination of factors, such as conflict and improving infrastructure, that provided the key motivation for movement.

The student is here focusing on the idea that it was ideology that drove expansion in the American West. The student quotes from two historians, Mary Norton and Frederick Jackson Turner, in support of this interpretation. The student then goes on to say that this opinion is not shared by all historians, and cites Donald Worster as an example of one who believes other factors were more important. These references are appropriately footnoted and listed in detail in the bibliography that the student submitted.

Qualities of a coherent and sustained argument

The qualities of a coherent and sustained argument are shown in the examples above. Both begin with an opinion:

- for Part A, Student 3 backs up the opinion using an in-depth evaluation of contemporary sources, supported by quoting a prominent historian
- for Part B, Student 4 shows evidence of wider reading, which is evaluated in support of – or to challenge – the author's opinion.

Moderators' notes

Many of the secondary sources will have been written by historians. You will need to show that you have followed and understood their points of view about your topic, especially when they differ.

Essential notes

'Manifest Destiny' was the ideological belief that white Americans were destined to occupy the whole of the USA, from the Atlantic to the Pacific Ocean.

Writing your conclusions

When thinking about your conclusion, remember to:

* summarise the main points in your argument
* reach a judgement that is supported by evidence of reading and by a strong working knowledge of the effects – long or short term – of the main issues.

Consider the focus and strengths of the following conclusions and think about how you are going to construct your own conclusion.

Example of a conclusion to a Part A enquiry

Student 5

Essential notes

The Suez crisis of 1956 occurred when the Egyptian leader, Colonel Gamal Abdul Nasser, announced his intention of nationalising the Suez Canal. This was a direct result of the USA cancelling a grant of $56 million towards the building of the Aswan Dam, a project Nasser believed would help Egypt's economy. Britain, frightened that Nasser intended to form some kind of Arab alliance to cut off oil supplies to Europe, formed a secret alliance with France and Israel and invaded Egypt. International pressure forced a cease-fire.

'How significant was the Suez crisis in influencing British policy towards Africa in the years after 1956?'

The Suez crisis was significant in that it demonstrated to the British that their role in international affairs was greatly diminished, and this impacted on the British Empire in Africa. The Suez crisis brought America into Africa, and this meant that Britain's policies toward Africa from then on had to converge with American views. The Suez crisis destroyed a British prime minister, greatly tested the Anglo–American alliance and played a significant role in influencing British policy, which led to the rapid contraction of Empire. However, most importantly, although Suez symbolised the end of the British Empire, it did not cause it; it was not critical in and of itself but was the point that brought these new realities into sharp focus. By exposing the underlying realities of a changed Anglo–American relationship, the inability of Britain to suppress growing nationalism and the changing patterns of trade and domestic priorities, the Suez crisis taught Britain a painful lesson in the realities of the new world order.

This student begins by making an overall inference – that Suez demonstrated Britain's diminished ability to influence international affairs. The student continues by pulling together the main points made in the body of the response, and concludes by returning to the initial inference, pointing up the symbolism of Suez. This is a good conclusion, leaving no doubt as to what the student believed was the short-term significance of the Suez crisis in influencing British policy toward Africa. However, this would have been better if one or two examples of how the policy was influenced by Suez had been given, although these were developed in the body of the response.

Example of a conclusion to a Part B enquiry
Student 6

> **'Assess the significance of the influence of American ideology on the process of the settlement of the West between 1789 and 1906.'**
>
> Once the West was opened up, it becomes a question of which factor played a key part in inspiring people to move and settle there, and it has been shown here that the underlying factor was that of ideology. Throughout the 19th century, the very idea of land entitlement was threaded through the history of the settlement of the West. Starting with the war of independence back in 1783, and built up through the Monroe Doctrine, the Louisiana Purchase, the Mexican war, the Homestead Act and through to the Battle of Wounded Knee, was belief in the idea that white settlers could take that which they believed to be theirs by right, and settle. Indeed, it was their manifest destiny to do so. It is true that developments such as barbed wire, wind pumps and railroads created opportunities for some in the West, and encouraged settlement there. However, the movement of a whole people could not have occurred so rapidly without the mindset and ideology that was created in white Americans, a sense of ownership that came from all these conflicts, infrastructural developments and government policies. Thus the influence of ideology was paramount in the process of the settlement of the West.

Essential notes

The Battle of Wounded Knee was between the US cavalry and the Lakota Sioux in December 1890. It is estimated that at least 300 Indians and 29 US troopers died. The battle effectively ended Indian resistance to white expansion.

This student is threading an understanding of the importance of ideology throughout the concluding paragraph. The student links the idea of land entitlement with a series of key events, developments and inventions that encouraged settlement. The student then returns to the ideology that underpinned the whole concept of land entitlement: that it was the 'manifest destiny' of the white American people to settle the West. This is a very good concluding paragraph.

Qualities of an effective conclusion
The above are examples of high calibre conclusions:

- each summarises the main points of their respective arguments
- Student 6 writes the better conclusion as it refers back more explicitly to the focus of the enquiry
- each conclusion shows strong evidence of the authors' respective judgements being supported by their reading and understanding of the issues.

Moderators' notes

Many students ask why they cannot simply write up their responses without a length restriction. In a written exam, you have to write to time. It is no good saying to the invigilator that you need another five minutes to finish off your answer properly. You have to develop the skill of writing to time. It is the same with coursework. You cannot simply write and write. You have to develop the skill of writing to length.

Moderators' notes

If your work is over the required length it will affect your overall mark quite badly, because the conclusion to your Part B enquiry is where you pull the whole enquiry together and make supported judgements (see page 75) and neither your teacher-moderator nor the Edexcel moderator will know what your final conclusions were.

Essential notes

Material in an appendix does not count towards the word limit.

Presenting your work

Writing to length

You have a maximum of 4000 words with which to work. You should try to divide these so that you write:

- 2000 words for Part A   (25 marks)
- 2000 words for Part B   (25 marks)

This is not a strict division. However, as you can see, because each part of your assignment is marked out of 25 marks, it would be sensible to keep as close as possible to 2000 words for each part.

Remember, too, that you have to put a cumulative word count at the foot of each page. This serves two purposes:

1. It helps you to keep tabs on how many words you have written.

2. It shows your teacher whether or not you have exceeded 4000 words overall.

Keeping to the word count

What happens if you write more than 4000 words?

- Your teacher will hand the assignment back to you and ask you to edit it so that the word total comes down to 4000.

- If this is not possible, for whatever reason, your teacher will stop marking your assignment once 4000 words have been read. This means that the last part of your Part B enquiry will not be marked.

Presenting your assignment

Finally, remember that you may either handwrite or word-process your assignment. However, for practical reasons, moderators suggest it is best to word-process the assignments. This makes it so much easier for you to organise your text. It also means the moderator will be able to clearly read your assignment.

Compiling a bibliography

You will have noticed that all the academic books you have read, as well as most textbooks, have a bibliography – either at the end of the book or after each chapter. You will need to compile a bibliography to show which books you have used in your assignment. This will consist of the books that appear in your resource record, as well as books that you have perhaps simply referred to in passing. Always put the books in alphabetical order, by author, surname first. Reference each book like this:

> Evans, Eric J., *The Forging of the Modern State 1783–1870*, published by Longman 1983 (3rd edition 2001)

Using an appendix

You may use an appendix for material that you have referred to in your response. You might, for example, have referred to a painting, a map or a speech. This can go in your appendix, and so can the sources that you are evaluating as part of your Part A enquiry.

Using endnotes and footnotes

Endnotes are a very useful way of referencing the source material you are
using when you write up your responses to the two enquiries. The best way of
describing how to do this is to give you an example. This comes from page 220
of the third edition of Eric J Evans's *The Forging of the Modern State 1783–1870* –
the book referenced in *Compiling a bibliography*, on page 76. Evans has put
these references at the end of a chapter entitled 'Class Consciousness?'

Notes and references

1. E. Hopkins *A Social History of the English Working Classes* (1979) p 197

2. E.P. Thompson 'The peculiarities of the English' *Socialist Register*
   (1965) pp 311–62

3. J.O. Foster Class *Struggle in the Industrial Revolution* (1964)

4. *The Democratic Review*, I (June 1849); *The Friend of the People* 11 Jan
   1851.

How has Eric Evans used these notes and references? When he has referred
to, or quoted from, for example, the book by E. Hopkins, he has put a little
number 1 in the text at the appropriate place. So it is easy, when reading
through the chapter, to see immediately where he has used these four
sources. You could reference your work in the same way. On the other hand,
you may like to reference in a slightly different way. Instead of putting all
the references at the end, as endnotes, you could put them at the foot of
each page as you write up your response. This example comes from Martin
Pugh, *The March of the Women*, published by Oxford University Press 2000.

On page 63 of this book, Pugh refers to three sources and numbers them 1–3 in
the body of his text. He references the sources at the foot of the page like this:

1. Lesley P. Hume, *The National Union of Women's Suffrage Societies,
   1897–1914* (New York: Garland Publishing, 1982), 3, suggests that after
   1884 the suffragists lost enthusiasm and the cause 'ceased to attract
   attention or adherents'; Andrew Rosen *Rise Up Women!* (*Routledge,
   1978*), 12, says that the period between 1884 and 1897 'marked the
   nadir of the women's suffrage movement'.

2. T. Billington-Greig, 'The Militant Policy of the Women Suffragists', 12
   Nov. 1906, Fawcett Library, Billington-Greig papers Box 404, file 3; E.
   Sylvia Pankhurst *The Suffragette Movement* (Virago 1977 edition), 92, 484.

3. Millicent Fawcett, 'Women's Suffrage: A Reply', *The Nineteenth
   Century*, 107 (1886), 746.

Here, you will see that Pugh has referred to two secondary works (1), two
contemporary pamphlets, one of which was re-published in 1977 (2), and
an article published in a 19th-century journal (3).

Moderators' notes

It is not compulsory to use
footnotes or endnotes. But
you will probably find it
easier to reference, in this
way, the sources you have
used. It will save words, too,
as words in the footnotes
aren't counted towards
the word limit. Remember,
though, that you may only use
footnotes in a fairly limited
way. You may use them
for attributions (giving the
title and author of a book
or article) and you may
use them for providing
identification (for example
saying that an individual was
Mayor of Birmingham). You
cannot use them to develop
your argument and make
further points.

Part A enquiry

How far did the Montgomery Bus Boycott improve equality for black people and the views of white people towards blacks 1955–65?

[25 marks]

This student is following a centre-designed coursework programme, *The USA: The African-American Experience from Civil War to Civil Rights 1865–1981.*

The topic of the enquiry is appropriate for the coursework programme and for a Part A enquiry. The word 'improve' is not quite right in the context of 'views of white people' because it all depends on your point of view as to whether 'views' have improved or not. The enquiry title would work better if the title read: *How far did the Montgomery Bus Boycott improve equality for black people and change the attitudes of white people towards blacks 1955–65?*

The student has used six contemporary sources:

1. *The Montgomery Advertiser*, 6 December 1955

2. A cartoon by Herblock, published in *The Washington Post* in 1956

3. A legal statement, dated 1956, about the purpose of the Browder versus Gayle case (referred to twice)

4. A YouTube clip of William Waheed explaining the importance of the Browder versus Gayle case

5. A quote by Martin Luther King contained in a high school essay on a US site, 'Kids for King'.

6. A quote by Roberta Wright about the outcome of the bus boycott.

They were all sourced from the internet and the student used footnotes to refer to the websites. The footnotes are not reproduced in this book.

There is nothing wrong in using the internet to search for contemporary sources. However, two things went awry with the way the sources were cited:

- The student simply gave the internet site as a reference, and not the document itself. It was therefore impossible for the moderator to know which documents the student had used without going to the sites and having a look. This is incredibly time-consuming and would not have to happen if the sources were properly referenced in the first place. Furthermore, YouTube was cited as a source and the site referenced was no longer available.
- Sources 5 and 6 are single line quotations. These are insufficient to enable the student to do a thorough source analysis.

Remember always to:

- reference the sources you use by giving the names of the actual documents
- make sure the written sources are long enough for you to undertake a thorough evaluation.

Grade C student answer

The Montgomery Bus Boycott was an incident that began on 1 December 1955 when Rosa Parks refused to give up her seat for a white person and was arrested. Until 20 December 1956 black people avoided using buses because of segregation laws on buses. I am going to assess how important and successful this event was in gaining equality and improving the opinion of white people towards blacks.

Rosa Parks refused to move seat on her bus when a white man entered. This highlighted the clear superiority that whites had in society. It also showed that white people saw black people as second-class citizens as they thought nothing of taking their seats. Because of the law of segregation on buses in the city, she was arrested and fined. Black people decided to boycott the buses. This was to help whites realise that black people refused to be treated like they were at this point. Black taxi drivers offered lifts for the same price as a bus and others helped by giving lifts to fellow blacks. However, the reaction of the newspapers wasn't so supportive.

Five days after the boycott began the *Montgomery Advertiser*'s articles weren't sympathetic towards Rosa and concentrated more on the violence blacks may have caused bus drivers. For example, it was alleged that a black person shot at a bus near Washington Park. This was the first story this article concentrated on, not that an innocent black woman was forced from her seat and arrested when she refused. The same article mentions that the bus authorities would continue to enforce the segregation laws, with drivers facing a penalty fine or sentence if they did not. This shows that in the immediate aftermath of the incident, black people weren't getting any more rights because the laws were still followed and not changed. This suggests that the authorities hadn't changed their opinion at all. This coming from a bus manager makes this source very reliable as it shows a clear opinion of those in charge. A week later, negroes met with bus officials asking for a first come first seated arrangement and black drivers to be hired on predominantly 'black routes'. This was refused as bus official Jack Crenshaw said it would be 'impossible to accept the proposed seating arrangement in view of the segregation law and the company has no intention of hiring black drivers.' A bus official saying this ☞

AO1 The student is here setting out, in a simple, straightforward way, the starting point for the enquiry. They are explaining what they are going to do. They then describe the event, which was Rosa Parks refusing to give up her seat on a segregated bus, and explain, briefly, the significance of this. If they had focused on the key issues involved here, their response would have been more analytical and they would have hit a higher level. As it is, this is a secure level 2.

AO2 An evaluation of contemporary source material is a very important component of a Part A enquiry, yet the student has here made no mention of the ways in which they intend to use this material. This should be done in an introduction.

AO2 The student is here focusing on the *Montgomery Advertiser* as a source, and has begun to evaluate it. They have described the evidence in *The Advertiser* rather than using direct quotes. Even so, they have gone behind looking at what it says (its surface features) and have begun to draw inferences from these surface features. They have put the *Montgomery Advertiser* into its historical context by relating it to the circumstances of the race laws that operated in Alabama. They have shown, too, something of the need to evaluate the source in the context of the values of Alabama. This paragraph would be assessed at low level 3, but the student could have improved their mark for AO2 by quoting directly from the sources and focusing more on the nature, origin and purpose of the source.

suggests that black people have no hope as they are in charge. This was proof that black people made hardly any progress in the initial stages of the boycott as they still were not seen as employable by bus companies and segregation laws prevented them from desegregating the buses.

Although the people in charge didn't seem to want to support blacks, many of the white public did. With no way of commuting for black people, many whites offered help by offering car pools. This shows that not all white people agreed with the opinion that blacks and whites should be segregated because they shared their cars with blacks. Also, it showed that not all whites saw black people as unequal. They were helping and supporting the cause for equality amongst blacks and whites. In that sense, the immediate aftermath of the Parks incident did have some positives. It highlighted the fact that some white people did support the fight for equality.

The cartoon[1] shows the effect the boycott had on bus companies and highlights a reason that the laws eventually changed. Before the boycott, the majority of bus riders were black. This means that during the boycott, bus companies were losing a lot of money. The image of an angry white bus manager losing his temper at a black man simply walking away shows how much it affected the bus companies. This cartoon could be suggesting that a change in laws was inevitable with bus officials becoming increasingly frustrated with the lack of income. However, this still shows that white people in general didn't support black people because they are only worried about losing money, not the rights of negroes. While taking away the profits of bus managers would help blacks become more equal, it wouldn't change the attitudes of white people. If anything, bus managers would be annoyed with blacks and think they are being a nuisance for not riding the bus, not thinking that they deserve equal rights. This is a problem with the boycott, many whites who agree with segregation and that whites are superior will think that blacks causing trouble and dislike them more.

The first major success of the boycott came in June 1956 with the Browder v. Gayle case. They ruled that current laws 'deny and deprive plaintiffs and other negro citizens similarly situated of the equal protection of the laws and due process of law secured by the Fourteenth Amendment.'[2] This was a great success in gaining equality for black people because the amendments of the ☞

AO1 The student has begun to tease out the key issues, and after focusing on the attitudes of the bus company and of the local press in supporting segregation legislation and has now begun to contrast this with the somewhat different attitudes of some white people. This is mixed up with description and so the paragraphs are only broadly analytical. The student is working at low level 3 for AO1 where the mark scheme rewards work that shows some understanding of the key issues related to the enquiry but which may include material which is descriptive. The student could have improved their mark if they had included less descriptive material and had concentrated more on drawing inferences from the issues they had spotted.

AO2 The student focuses immediately on the cartoon, and gives a very direct response to it and to what it demonstrates about white people's attitude to the boycott. The mark scheme would say that it is interpreted with confidence – they don't mess about! In interpreting the cartoon, the student puts it into the context of the Montgomery Bus Boycott, but not into the broader context of Alabama and the segregation laws.

AO1 The student is using the cartoon to show that what was uppermost in people's minds was their take-home pay, not the rights of black people. The link between this and black equality should have been more clearly made and evidence provided in support. Greater attention should have been paid to grammar. The next to last sentence, for example, is a bit muddled and could well be split into two. This paragraph would be assessed at low level 3.

United States proved that they deserved equality. Browder v. Gayle was hugely important. It proved that it was unlawful to treat black people this way. William Waheed, who was a part of the civil rights movement, explains the importance here.[3] He says, 'the situation with the bus was a tactic that racial segregation is used to demean black people.' He suggests that blacks were okay with separation as long as they were equal but this was used against black people and they had to fight it. Whites were taking advantage of negroes within the Jim Crow laws and Browder v. Gayle proved them to be wrong. However, segregation on buses was not ended yet. This video is the opinion of a man there at the time and he knew exactly what was going on so he knows what he's talking about making it reliable.

The actual end of this case came on 13 November 1956 and signified that segregation on buses were unconstitutional. The ruling: 'The supremacy of the federal government in matters affecting interstate commerce is axiomatic. Cases involving the exercise of its power in that realm shed no light on Fourteenth Amendment problems. It does seem quite clear that by its terms the Congress is given the power and duty to enforce the Fourteenth Amendment by legislation. Thus the Congress would have the power, thus derived, to proscribe segregation in intrastate transportation.'[4] This source is very reliable as it is a document from the original trial so cannot be argued with. This was a great step towards equality for black people and their first real victory over segregation. Their boycott had ultimately been successful in gaining equality. The boycott then officially ended a week later when the law that stated that black could sit virtually wherever they wanted came through. This was obviously a great victory for black people but would white people react well to this?

During the boycott many white people reacted angrily. While some helped by offering lifts to blacks and taxi drivers reduced fares, some white people weren't so supportive. Martin Luther King's house was even bombed. The government tried hard to halt the boycott as it cost the city lots of money. This wasn't good in building relations between blacks and whites. The government even said that the boycott was illegal and arrested Dr King. This didn't improve the views of whites towards blacks because they were trying everything in their power to prevent black authority. However, ☞

AO1 The student here has identified, and is focusing on, a key issue, the Browder v. Gayle case. Whilst the approach is analytical, it is not too clear what the case was about. This needs to be more sharply explained and then the analysis will follow more securely.

It should also be noted that the student slightly misinterprets Mr Waheed's message and his role (he is a filmmaker, not a civil rights worker, and his quotation in context was expressing the reasons why people were protesting at the time).

AO2 It is not altogether clear what the source is that the student is evaluating, but it seems to be the YouTube clip. They could have improved their evaluation by paying much more attention to the nature, origin and purpose of the source. Their conclusion in the last sentence of the first paragraph that 'he was there at the time and he knew exactly what was going on so he knows what he's talking about making it reliable' is simplistic. This would be assessed at high level 2 or low level 3.

AO1 The student is here exploring the wider short-term impact of the boycott, contrasting government reaction and that of individuals in a broadly analytical paragraph that needs greater depth and development to achieve above a level 3.

despite these attempts and the angry reaction of some whites, the boycott did gain a lot of support. A lot was due to Dr King's non-violent protests and the way he reacted to events such as his house being bombed as he once said, 'Be calm as I and my family are. We are not hurt and remember that if anything happens to me, there will be others to take my place.'[5] White people saw the boycott as this non-violence and got behind them. People all over the country held non-violent protests of their own, by collecting money and holding prayer meetings, clearly influenced by the boycott. This shows that the boycott helped improve the opinion of whites towards blacks because they helped out by collecting money.

The aftermath of the bus boycott showed that there were still problems. Snipers were shot at buses when blacks returned. This shows that the opinions of blacks had not completely improved as some white people were out to get them. The KKK gained more influence and were out to get blacks, using violence. Extremist groups like this proved that not all was well between whites and blacks. However, the KKK eventually lost some of its power. The violence died down after some white people spoke out against it and integration on buses was ultimately successful. This showed improved relations as before no one from the white community really spoke out against segregation and civil rights of black people. As a result of the boycott, the SCLC was founded in January 1957, with Martin Luther King Jr as president. The lasting legacy of the boycott, as Roberta Wright wrote, was that 'it helped to launch a 10-year national struggle for freedom and justice, the Civil Rights Movement that stimulated others to do the same at home and abroad.'[6] This is one woman's view so can't be seen as completely reliable but in many ways she is right, it was a struggle but over the next ten years black people gained lots more equality. Many white people realised that blacks deserved equality and supported. While there was a lot of violence, such as a black teenager getting attacked as she exited a bus, they were the result of a minority of whites. These extremists didn't represent the true opinion of all white people any more. ☞

AO2 Although a relevant quote from Martin Luther King has been used, it is not long enough or substantial enough to be properly evaluated. Two sentences do not give enough for the nature and purpose of the source to be really thoroughly drawn out and detailed inferences to be drawn. The quote, however, is appropriately contextualised and simple inferences drawn from it. This would be assessed at level 2.

AO1 The student is here developing the broader short-term significance of the Montgomery Bus Boycott. They are beginning to consider the impact of the boycott on the development of the KKK and on the founding of the SCLC. Raising these issues makes it a broadly analytical response. The focus is clear and shows a good understanding of these key issues. It would be assessed at high level 3.

AO2 Just like the quote from Martin Luther King, the quotation from Roberta Wright is barely sufficient to stand effective evaluation as a source. What, for example, is its origin and purpose? Roberta Wright is not identified and so there is no way that what she says can be evaluated for reliability. The quotation is evaluated at a very basic level, contextualised and cross-referenced to the student's own knowledge. This would be assessed at low level 2.

In conclusion, the equality of black people improved greatly as a result of the Montgomery Bus Boycott. On buses in the city, blacks and whites were integrated as a result of the boycott and also the important Browder v. Gayle case, which deemed the previous laws unconstitutional. The ruling of that case, which ended the boycott, was successful for black people gaining civil rights. It made integrated city buses, they could sit where they liked and not move when a white person entered. However, one of the main reasons bus managers agreed to these laws was because it lost them lots of money. In that sense, it could be argued that whites were still against blacks and still thought of them as unequal, added to the emergence of extremist groups who attacked blacks getting off of buses and snipers being shot at buses when the blacks returned to the buses in December 1956, the boycott could be seen as unsuccessful in improving the attitude of white people towards blacks. However, this is not true. Many white people supported the boycott by holding prayer groups, collecting money and offering lifts to black people who previously rode buses. Taxi drivers even reduced fares to help. In the aftermath of the boycott, many whites stood up to others who attacked innocent blacks. This never happened before so it showed an improvement of what many white people thought of blacks. In the long term, this boycott was the beginning of a ten-year struggle for complete civil rights for black people. Despite the best efforts of extremist groups and local government, black people achieved a lot more equality and improved relations with many white people.

A clear conclusion to the enquiry, focusing well on the short-term significance of the Montgomery Bus Boycott. The importance of the Black Movement and the use of law are emphasised, whilst at the same time making clear that economics were paramount throughout. The importance of the state, individual white supporters of the boycott and extremists are also considered and a supported judgement reached. ☞

Endnotes

1. A cartoon by Herblock, published in *The Washington Post*, 1956

2. A legal statement, dated 1956, about the purpose of the Browder v. Gayle case.

3. A YouTube clip of William Waheed explaining the importance of the Browder v. Gayle case

4. A legal statement, dated 1956, about the purpose of the Browder v. Gayle case

5. A quote by Martin Luther King contained in a high school essay on a US site 'Kids for King'

6. A quote by Roberta Wright about the outcome of the bus boycott

AO1 A response relating well to the focus of the enquiry, which is the short-term significance of the Montgomery Bus Boycott. The student has identified relevant key issues, but because there is some descriptive material the response is only broadly analytical. The factual material included is all relevant to the enquiry, although there is some imbalance in its selection, which focuses a little too much on the boycott itself. The conclusion is strong.

Most of the skills needed to produce a convincing account of the results of an enquiry are demonstrated, although not all paragraphs are well organised.

This response is worthy of a **high level 3 for AO1 and would gain 10 out of 13 marks**.

AO2 A range of source material has been selected, which relates well to the enquiry. Most of the sources are generally interpreted with confidence and related well to their historical context. There is some evidence of evaluation for reliability and utility. However, the evaluation of two sources is cursory, and the student would have done well to have focused on an in-depth evaluation of fewer sources or to have made Sources 5 and 6 much stronger.

This response is worthy of a **low level 3 for AO2 and would gain 8 out of 12 marks**.

QoWC The Quality of written communication matches the quality of the historical understanding shown.

Overall, this response would gain **18 marks**.

Part A enquiry

What was the short-term significance of Pearl Harbor for international relations in the years to 1945?

[25 marks]

This student is following the Edexcel-designed coursework programme, *CW40: International Relations 1879–1980.*

The title is written so that it is well-phrased and focuses on short-term significance. It is also appropriate for the coursework programme being followed by the student.

The student has used nine contemporary sources. They were all presented in an appendix. The sources and appendix are not reproduced in this book.

1. President Roosevelt's speech to the American nation on 8 December 1941

2. American newspaper, the *Seattle Post Intelligencer*, 9 December 1941

3. British cartoon 'All present and correct, Ma'am', by David Lowe, published in the *Evening Standard*, 9 December 1941

4. British cartoon 'Revenge!', by Leslie Illingworth, published in the *Daily Mail*, 11 December 1941 (Appendix 4)

5. British cartoon 'Lest we forget', by Sidney 'George' Strube, published in the *Daily Express*, 7 December 1941

6. White House press release announcing the bombing of Hiroshima, 6 August 1945

7. Extract from a letter written by Admiral Yamamoto in reply to one from Hiroyuki Agawa

8. Comment by Admiral Hara Tadaichi

9. Comment made by Prime Minister Winston Churchill after the bombing of Pearl Harbor

The student has chosen a wide range of sources, all of which are relevant to the enquiry. However, nine is probably too many to manage a sufficiently effective evaluation of them all, and the inclusion of three cartoons is perhaps too many. However, it may well be that the student is going to focus more sharply on a smaller number of sources as far as in-depth evaluation is concerned, and use some simply to illustrate points being made.

Remember always to cite your sources in footnotes or endnotes. The style of references used can vary as long as the source of information is accurately cited.

Grade A* student answer

December 1941: the world had been brought together within the second global conflict of the century. The axis powers were heading towards global dominance, having successfully invaded much of Europe and the Low Countries, leaving an isolated Britain and distanced Soviet Union to balance the international scene. The war would seemingly be decided by a straight German–Russian offensive. However, the events of 7 December 1941 arguably acted as the defining moment of the Second World War, an event that would have notable implications for the balance of power on the international stage and the future of many countries for the forthcoming years.

Pearl Harbor held great significance across international affairs as it signalled the introduction of the mass military strength of America into the Second World War, a defining moment in the conflict. This view is supported by Christopher Culpin,[1] who suggests that Pearl Harbor ended America's reluctance to enter the war in one crucial blow. The decision to place the USA directly in a state of war with Japan was reflected in, and on the face of it, initiated by, President Roosevelt's address to America[2] the following day. Roosevelt's speech, containing both power and substance, was ignited by the first line: 'a day that will live in infamy', and explicitly contemplated the significance of the event for the future of the USA. With frequent references to the impact: 'understand the implications to the very life and safety of our nation', Roosevelt makes obvious his desire to extinguish the threat of Japanese aggression, first to preserve the safety of America and second to allow the allied powers to emerge victorious. Roosevelt's frequent use of personal pronouns, such as 'our' and 'we', directly and collectively refer to the American population. The motives behind the speech could be numerous: an attempt to reassure, to motivate and, crucially, to mobilise support for imminent war. In addressing the entire country, the content may have been exaggerated in order to fulfil purposes of motivation, especially at a time of great uncertainty for the American population, ultimately appeasing them. The speech appears to be a deliberate response, at this time of ambiguity, to appease the public. Ultimately, all these factors attempt to justify America's entrance into the war. The source is dependable as it summarises the mutual feeling of the majority of Americans and ☞

This is a good, clear introduction, stating how, in December 1941, planes from the Japanese air force attacked the US Pacific fleet as it was moored at the US base in Pearl Harbor, Hawaii. The student is setting the scene by putting the Japanese attack on Pearl Harbor appropriately into the context of the Second World War, and suggesting its significance.

AO1 The student is here focusing confidently on the immediate short-term significance of the Japanese attack on Pearl Harbor, showing a good understanding of the main key issue, which was to catapult the USA into the Second World War, and in particular an understanding of the diversity of Roosevelt's motives.

This paragraph is focused on the first contemporary source selected by the student. They go straight into the source itself, and 'unpack' it, looking at the tone of the phrases and inferences that can be drawn from them. They then look at the source as a whole and consider it as evidence of the USA's motives at that time. This means it is interrogated confidently. The evidence derived from this interrogation is evaluated as to the historical significance of the event. This is supported by reference to a modern historian. The source is evaluated and analysed for nature, origin and purpose and demonstrates an appropriate understanding of the values of society at the time.

The student is operating at level 4 on both assessment objectives.

Roosevelt's attempt to meet these fears. Underpinning the message throughout is the extent to which America would go to gain revenge.

The Pearl Harbor attack, alongside Roosevelt's speech, were reported to the US public largely through national newspapers such as the *Seattle Post Intelligencer*.[3] The front page attempts to convey the shock that Pearl Harbor generated across America by the use of commanding titles that reflect the perceived injustice of the event, this being a technique used to fuel future support by reflecting negatively on Pearl Harbor. Despite seemingly attempting to remain neutral, the possibility of an ulterior motive cannot be underestimated, particularly with this being an American-based newspaper, which would probably have American interests at hand. For example, the quote 'electrified nation immediately unites for a terrific struggle ahead' promotes and almost advertises the war to America. This may have been the will of the President in order to influence recruitment for the conflict that lay ahead. Despite alternative motives, the inclusion of factual statistics adds legitimacy to the information and consequently improves dependability: '104 known dead and more than 800 wounded'. This article is thus dependable to a certain extent as the motive, stirring up support for war, probably lay behind the techniques used to present the information.

American entry into the war coincided with a flourish of nationalism and mobilisation of efforts toward the war, as illustrated by a cartoon by David Lowe published in the newspaper the *Evening Standard*.[4] The cartoon shows a British and an American officer, together, saluting the Statue of Liberty. The words: 'United 100 per cent war basis' are included, suggesting the alliance was at its optimum strength and fully oriented and focused for the war ahead with both countries '100 per cent' geared for success. The strength of both countries proved superior to Japan's, a view supported by historian A.J.P. Taylor[5] who concurs that the allies' focus and superior capability proved decisive in the conflict. Historian Robin Cross[6] reiterates that Pearl Harbor invigorated a tide of nationalism and unity that prompted revenge. The Statue of Liberty represents a founding image of the freedoms America and Britain stood for and which were endangered by Pearl Harbor; the cartoon implies that both countries will do their utmost to safeguard these, thus concentrating all resources available for the war effort as two beacons of freedom standing together. This source supports ☞

AO1 The student is focusing on the key issue of the dissemination of information; greater development here, such as a comparison with other methods of spreading information, would have made for a more secure level 4.

The student is here analysing the nature and purpose of the second source selected, the *Seattle Post Intelligencer*. They consider the motives that lay behind the article, and cross-reference to their perceived understanding of how President Roosevelt would have wanted the press to report the attack on Pearl Harbor. Their evaluation of the evidence takes account of the nature, origin and purpose of the source. The student shows an understanding of the need to evaluate the evidence in its historical context; the aftermath of the attack on Pearl Harbor.

AO1 This paragraph focuses confidently on a key issue – that of resurgent nationalism – and is supported by well-selected factual material.

AO2 The cartoon is interpreted well. The student looks at its component parts and draws inferences from them. In order to support these inferences, they cross-reference for support to two historians, A.J.P. Taylor and Robin Cross. In reaching a judgement, the status of the evidence is considered by commenting on the appearance of the cartoon in the newspaper the *Evening Standard* and on the conclusions that could be drawn from that with regard to the likelihood of the cartoon reflecting typical attitudes regarding resurgent nationalism.

President Roosevelt's speech and is dependable as it conveys the extent to which America was committed to the war effort and wanted to emerge successful. The political stance of the *Evening Standard*, however, needs to be considered. Traditionally right-wing, its content could attempt to appease readers, with views of a nationalistic nature. Potentially it was in the newspaper's interest, politically, to stir up support for the war.

Revenge emerged as a further short-term significance, illustrated by a cartoon drawn by Leslie Illingworth[7] and published in the *Daily Mail* on 11 December 1941. The cartoon emphasises the extent to which both countries were driven by revenge, with coffins covered in British and American national flags, emphasised by the British and American individuals standing behind, crossing their swords in the air. Liddell Hart[8] concurs in confirming that retaliation to Pearl Harbor motivated the USA raid on Tokyo in 1942. The cartoon references acts of Japanese aggression with Pearl Harbor listed below the American coffin, reiterating that this was the reason behind America's quest for revenge. Pearl Harbor could, however, be seen to bear less significance regarding Britain's response with the cartoon listing the *Prince of Wales* and the *Repulse*, battleships sunk by the Japanese in an unrelated incident, implying that the reasoning behind Britain's revenge were the acts of aggression aimed directly at them such as the invasion of Malaya rather than the attack on Pearl Harbor. Nevertheless, Pearl Harbor strengthened Britain's desire for revenge by providing a further incentive to unite with America as shown by individuals representing both countries standing shoulder to shoulder. A connection between nationalism and revenge, as the two main short-term significances show, is established through the similarities between this and the Lowe cartoon.

The significance of America's contribution to the course of the war is highlighted by Sidney Strube through a publication in the *Daily Express*,[9] a year after the attack on Pearl Harbor. The cartoon illustrates the shift in dominance globally between America and Japan with an American sailor threatening the Japanese prime minister, with his bayonet piercing a document reading 'December 7th'. This firstly strengthens the previous point that Pearl Harbor held significance regarding revenge, with the cartoon implying that Pearl Harbor was the motivation behind America's action. Secondly, the cartoon reflects the impact America had on the war. Both points 👉

AO1 A further key issue, that of revenge, is considered and analysed, supported by well-selected factual material. Again, the student has related the cartoon to events (the sinking of the *Repulse* and the invasion of Malaya) that could have given the British cause for revenge and linked these to the perceived American desire for revenge after the Pearl Harbor attack.

AO2 The cartoon is interrogated and analysed: the student has taken the component parts of the cartoon and drawn inferences from them as well as looking at the cartoon as a whole and considering it as evidence for the revenge motive. The judgements made are supported by accurate factual material and by cross-referencing to the Lowe cartoon.

AO1 The student is effectively developing the key issue of revenge by demonstrating an understanding of the shifting balance of power once the USA joined the war by accurate reference to the Pacific campaign in general and the Battle of the Coral Sea in particular.

are justified and the source proved dependable by the Pacific campaign that the allied powers ventured into following the attack on Pearl Harbor. The Pacific war had turned in favour of the allies with successful battles at Coral Sea (May 1942) and midway (June 1942) shifting the ascendancy from Japan to the allied powers. The balance of power had shifted from Japan to America, as illustrated by the source, and with further offences in Guadalcanal and Burma, it highlighted the amplified military capability of America and Britain. Liddell Hart[10] agrees that America's contribution to the war was telling in declaring that their introduction turned the tide in the Pacific.

America's search for revenge held further significance as it indirectly linked Pearl Harbor to the nuclear bombs of Hiroshima and Nagasaki. President Truman's direct reference to Pearl Harbor in his address to Congress[11] (on 6 August 1945) following the bombings highlighted this, implying that revenge was very much the base reasoning: 'the Japanese began the war from the air at Pearl Harbor'. America ultimately blamed Japan for their involvement in the war and hence highlighted revenge as the objective behind Hiroshima and Nagasaki. Hiroshima and Nagasaki not only drove Japan to surrender but also confirmed that revenge had been satisfied by ensuring that Pearl Harbour would never happen again: 'Let there be no mistake, we shall completely destroy Japan's power to make war.' The speech possesses similarities to that of President Roosevelt, discussed earlier, in terms of dependability and in being that ulterior motives could be plentiful. Broadcast to the American public, the speech content may be intended to appease the public rather than provide the truth. Instead of revenge being the motive behind the speech, Truman may have wished firmly to establish America as a global superpower, illustrating America's dominance on the international stage in an emphatic manner. Therefore Pearl Harbor may not be directly related to the nuclear bombings. However, Truman having revenge as a motive is directly supported by Peter Calvocoressi,[12] who believed that the humiliation inflicted on America at Pearl Harbor played a paramount role in the decisions made at Hiroshima and Nagasaki.

According to Japanese admirals, Pearl Harbor had damning consequences for the future of Japan. Admiral Yamamoto and Tadaichi interpreted the tactical attack on Pearl Harbor as the reason for Japan's defeat in the war. Admiral Yanamoto explained: 'A military man can scarcely pride himself on having smitten a sleeping enemy,'[13] ☞

AO2 The student here interrogates the source confidently by addressing its component parts and so identifying issues. Judgements are supported by referencing back to the previous paragraph where the revenge motive is first mentioned, and supported by accurate factual material.

On both assessment objectives, the student is working within level 4.

AO1 The student is here focusing confidently on the period 1941–5, which is important because this is the timeframe of the enquiry, and is linking Roosevelt's speech to the bombings of Hiroshima and Nagasaki.

The student is analysing President Truman's speech to Congress four years after Pearl Harbor and is showing some very effective cross-referencing, linking his speech back to the Japanese attack on Pearl Harbor and to Roosevelt's speech (the first source). The judgements arising from the source evaluation are well supported by historians' interpretations.

The student is working at level 4 on both objectives.

acknowledging that Pearl Harbor brought isolationist America, the greatest power in the world at the time, into the war against its will and now wanting to direct all its revenge against Japan. This opinion is supported by Dave Flitton[14] who declares that Pearl Harbor was overwhelmingly Japan's greatest military mistake of World War Two. Therefore Pearl Harbor resulted in a heavily defeated Japan, a view with which Admiral Tadaichi concurs: 'We won a great victory at Pearl Harbor and thereby lost the war.'[15] These quotes are dependable as expressions of opinions at the time; these individuals were in a position to understand the overall situation. They both held high ranks at the time of the Pearl Harbor operation and were in a position to have an accurate knowledge and understanding of Japan's military strength and capability. Such comments would not be made to rally the public in support, but rather to state starkly the true logistics of the situation.

In conclusion, Pearl Harbor resulted in notable significances, not just in influencing the short-term futures of Britain, Japan and America but ultimately the world globally and on the relationships between countries. The most notable short-term significance was the introduction of the USA into the war, a direct consequence of Pearl Harbor, which changed the direction of the war and enabled the allies to emerge victorious. American involvement signified a full-scale world war as A.J.P. Taylor[16] concurred, by suggesting the circle had been completed. Pearl Harbor fuelled considerable feelings of nationalism and revenge, and boasted a connection with the bombings of Hiroshima and Nagasaki and, effectively, Japanese surrender. America's decision to adopt an interventionist policy was the major short-term significance to emerge from Pearl Harbor. As Winston Churchill said when the USA entered the war: 'So we had won after all! As for the Japanese, they would be ground to powder.'[17]

Endnotes

1. Culpin, Christopher, *Making History: World History from 1914 to the Present Day*, 1984 (page 137)

2. See Appendix 1

3. See Appendix 2

4. See Appendix 3

5. Taylor, A.J.P., *The Second World War: an Illustrated History*, Penguin books, 1974 (page 13) ☞

AO1 The student has a clear focus in this paragraph, linking the bombing of Pearl Harbor to Hiroshima and Nagasaki.

AO2 The student is here showing some effective cross-referencing of the comments made by the Japanese Admirals to the attack on Pearl Harbour and supports this by reference to historian Flitton in support of judgements made. The use of fewer sources might have enabled a deeper evaluation to have been made and, although this is assessed at level 4, it could have achieved a higher level if this had been done.

A brief conclusion, but effectively summarising the short-term significance of Pearl Harbor and linking it to the British reaction and the outcome of the war.

6. Cross, Robin, *World War II in Photographs*, 2009 (page 95)

7. See Appendix 4

8. Hart, Liddell, *History of the Second World War*, Papermac, 1970 (page 359)

9. See Appendix 5

10. Hart, Liddell, *History of the Second World War*, Papermac, 1970 (page 359)

11. See Appendix 6

12. Calvocoressi, Peter, *World Politics since 1945*, Second edition, 1971 (page 3)

13. See Appendix 7

14. As quoted in *Battlefield,* a war documentary (TV series), Series 4, Episode 4, directed by Dave Flitton (Time-Life Cromwell Productions Ltd)

15. See Appendix 8

16. Taylor A.J.P., *The Second World War: an Illustrated History*, Penguin books, 1974 (page 124)

17. See Appendix 9

AO1 An analytical response, which relates well to the focus of the question. It focuses confidently on the significance of Pearl Harbor, and shows a good understanding of the key issues, with an evaluation of the relevant arguments. The analysis is supported by well-selected factual material that is completely relevant to the focus of the enquiry.

The writing is controlled, with each paragraph focused on a separate issue, and explains the results of the enquiry in a logical, coherent way.

This response is worthy of a **high level 4 for AO1 and would gain 12 out of 13 marks.**

AO2 The question is thoroughly investigated using a range of appropriate sources. The evidence from the sources is integrated well into a structured and sustained argument. The evidence is confidently interrogated, and its interpretation and evaluation takes account of the nature, origin and purpose of the sources. It shows an understanding of the need to explore the implications of the evidence within their historical context and also within the context of the values and assumptions of the society from which they are drawn. In reaching supported judgements, the status of the evidence is considered. This response is worthy of a **high level 4 for AO2 and would gain the full 12 marks.**

QoWC The quality of written communication matches the quality of the historical understanding shown.

Overall, this response would achieve **24 marks**.

Part B enquiry

Assess the significance of the influence of infrastructure developments for the process of the settlement of the West, 1789–1906.

[25 marks]

This student is following a centre-designed programme, *The USA: the Making of a Nation 1789–1906*.

The enquiry title is appropriate for the coursework programme being followed, spans the entire timeframe of that programme and focuses on change over time, using infrastructure developments as a factor to be compared with alternative factors in determining which was the most important in the process of change over time. It would seem, however, that the phrase 'of the influence' is redundant. The enquiry title would work better if it read: '*Assess the significance of infrastructure developments for the process of the settlement of the West during 1789–1906.*'

Grade C student answer

The spread of the American territory westwards was a long and sometimes slow process, which took well over a century to fully occur. Over this time certain factors helped speed the process up; some such as wars helped America acquire new land and therefore helped the American expansion to spread from coast to coast. The movement of people to the west was a slower process than that of gaining new land; settlement was encouraged in various ways, from new government policies introduced, to new infrastructures being created. Encouraging people to move from settled homes into relatively unknown and 'wild' west was always going to be difficult but extremely important in completing America's vision of being a country that stretched from east coast to west. Specific government policies were set up to actively encourage permanent residence in the west such as the Homestead Act of 1862. Individuals such as Polk, who was an active encourager of the move west, was instrumental in acquiring land and spreading the message of fulfilling the American 'Manifest Destiny' of moving westwards. However, if the infrastructure in the west had not been in place, then the settlement of people could never have happened. There has to be an accessible route and facilities for people to be able to move, before people can champion the idea. ☞

AO1 An introduction that shows clearly the student understands that many factors were involved in the process of settling the West. A broad range of appropriate factors has been suggested, demonstrating an understanding of the key issues involved.

The student clearly understands that the range of factors identified here operated at different rates and speeds in order to bring about change in the expansion of the USA. These factors are in turn linked to the major issue of settlement and the need for government policies to encourage this. Finally, the student pulls this all together by explaining the key importance of the presented factor: the importance of infrastructure.

Without infrastructure in an area, settlement is very hard. For people to uproot and start new communities there needs to be a foundation for them to build upon. The 2000 mile route known as the Oregon Trail[1] was one of the earlier infrastructural developments. The route led to many Americans uprooting and moving with the prospect of better agricultural land. Marcus Whitman told of a country of almost unbelievable fertility.[2] The trail was only significant in settlement towards the late 1830s and after, by 1845 5000 Americans were living in Oregon.[3] As early as the 1840s the need for a railroad was recognised. The construction of the transcontinental railroads were not sanctioned until 1862 and then another line in 1864, the government were, however, fully behind the idea. They offered lots of financial incentives to get the tracks up and running and more importantly offered land around the track to encourage settlement and development on the land. 'Each mile of track laid received from $16 000 to $48 000 in government bonds plus 20 square miles of land along a 400 foot wide right of way.'[4] As well as the land around the area being used for infrastructures and settlements, the railroads made the west more accessible, whole families could move away, but yet could still communicate with the home they had left. Boyer backs up the idea that the railroads had direct links with movement westwards: 'In short, the railroads accelerated development in the west.'[5] They also had influence on agriculture farmers could move with their animals to the west; however, barbed wire had the most dramatic effect on agriculture. The most popular style of farming before the invention of barbed wire in 1873 was ranching; the farmers did not have one settled home and most were young single men. 'Barbed wire proved a cheap and durable means of enclosure.'[6] It encouraged a permanent base and a more family orientated farm. In 1880 alone $80.5m worth of barbed wire was produced.[7] The developments and improvements in the infrastructure in the west was significant in bringing about settlement, they actively encouraged and helped settlement of people in the west increase. It considerably raised the number of permanent locations of farmers alongside the Homestead Act. The fact that only farmers really seemed to benefit from development of barbed wire was a limitation of infrastructural developments, it did not really increase the diversity of those settling westwards. ☞

AO1 The student is here focusing on the presented factor: infrastructure. However, the student is mixing up some analysis with some descriptive material. This means that the enquiry is straying from its overall focus, which is on assessing significance. In mark scheme terms, the paragraph is only broadly analytical. Furthermore, this is the only paragraph focusing on the presented factor, and yet the student is not extending it to cover the whole chronological range of the coursework programme (1789–1906) but is focusing almost exclusively on the 19th century. It is not always factually accurate (such as the invention of barbed wire) and shows some confusion between farmers, cowboys and ranchers.

This is work within level 3, but would be assessed towards the bottom of the level because of the quality of written communication (see below).

Quality of Written Communication The student clearly has a good working knowledge of the importance of infrastructure, but is finding organising ideas a bit challenging. This paragraph would have been clearer if it had been broken up into several shorter ones, each targeted on a specific aspect of the importance of infrastructure. Several sentences, too, are very long and different ideas are separated by a comma when a new sentence should have begun.

If the government had not been supportive of the full expansion and settlement of the west it may never have occurred when it did. One of the earliest signs of the government's intentions towards America being from coast to coast was the Munroe Doctrine; in 1823 President Monroe outlined the country stance on European intervention on the continent of America. America's stance of isolation was reinforced towards Europe 'not to interfere in the internal concerns of any of its powers'[8]w hich was a stance they tried to maintain for many years. The Doctrine threatened war if any European state was to interfere, this gave the American people a sense of unity, fighting for their land against a common enemy, in addition, 'it tapped American nationalism and anti-British and anti-European feelings.'[9] It was an essentially nationalistic declaration[10] that helped embed the idea of westward expansion, and that it was America's destiny to stretch from coast to coast. The Doctrine did not necessarily help western settlement it had more significance in western expansion and the obtaining of land. The Homestead Act of 1862 however had a big impact on permanent settlement. Noy supports this: 'the act did spur settlement of the west and served as a powerful symbolic statement of the government's intentions to fulfil Manifest Destiny'.[11] The act allowed farmers to gain land in the west, by one of two methods. One include a five year stay and the land became theirs or the second a six month stay and they pay a fee ($1.25 per acre) either method helped encourage movement to the new lands in the west. Between 1862 and 1900, 600 000 settlers claimed their homesteads.[12] Problems did occur with the Act, the terrain in parts of the land up for homesteading was incredibly poor and unsuitable for farming. The government reacted by introducing further policies such as the Desert Land Act of 1877, and then the Timber and Stone Act a year later, which gave even more incentive for people to move west. There were other problems too, the system was abused, with big companies taking large areas of land and making a hefty profit, even when the normal American farmer got the land there were often high failure rates. In Nebraska the failure rate of a homestead was 43%.[13] All the government policies from across the period show the government's intentions for expansion and settlement across the continent. The Monroe Doctrine had a much greater effect on expansion rather than settlement, but arguably without the expansion ☞

AO1 This very long paragraph focuses on the first alternative factor identified by the student – that of government action. The student has identified key issues involved: the Munroe Doctrine, the Homestead Act of 1862 and the Desert Land Act of 1877 and does tease out the significance of these in descriptive passages. There is some analysis showing an understanding of the nature of change over time. However, the student is again focusing on the 19th century instead of the whole period of the coursework programme. This, together with the previous paragraph, is beginning to create a chronological imbalance in the response as a whole. This is work within level 3, but would be assessed towards the bottom of the level because of the quality of written communication.

the settlement could not have taken place. 'The Homestead Act did allow small-scale settlement to develop'[14] but had failings with its corruption and high numbers of unsuccessful purchases.

Wars and conflicts were a way in which lots of land was gained by the USA; they fought various races to gain and retain land that rightfully they felt was theirs. The war of 1812 was not significant in land gained (only westerly parts of Florida) but the war had effects on the mood of the nation and their attitudes towards westward settlement. 'The war inspired a great outburst of national feeling in a still feeble union.'[15] These feelings would later become similar to Polk's idea of 'Manifest Destiny'. The war showed that the American people were willing to unite for their country as nearly 30 000 troops took up arms,[16] but as well as this the war of 1812 had an impact on the removal of the Indians. 'Tecumseh's death and Jackson's defeat at Creeks crippled Indian power east of Mississippi and facilitated Western settlement.[17] TheM exican-American war 1846–8 was a much more significant war for settlement as well as expansion of territory. The war led to the Treaty of Guadalupe-Hidalgo, which meant that Texas and California were now part of America. The acquisition of Texas brought about some problems later on, between slave and non-slave states which led to the Civil War, but California brought about the Gold Rush of 1849. When gold was discovered in California a gold fever spread across the country and abroad enticing young men to come seek their fortunes in the Californian mines. The Gold Rush brought a high number of short-term settlers to the west, but because most came on their own, very few communities were established, although the city of San Francisco emerged from the demand that the miners created. Another conflict important to Indian removal was Wounded Knee in 1890; on 29 December 300 Indians including seven infants were slaughtered.[18] The death of these 300 Indian people brought about the end of many years of fighting over land with the Indians; with them removed the land was now free for white Americans to settle in. Such was the reduction of the Indians that by 1900 the plain Indian population had shrunk from nearly a quarter of a million to just over 100 000.[19] The importance of conflict in America being what it is today cannot be underestimated, after all if the land was never gained, then no settlement could ever happen. However, the direct significance of war on settlement on the west was minimal the impact was on expansion. ☞

AO1 The student is here focusing on a second alternative factor: wars and conflict. There is some analysis at the beginning of the paragraph, but much of this is descriptive work. There is some loss of focus on the question, particularly towards the end. However, the student has made a real effort to cover the whole time span and so provide chronological balance. To improve their mark the student needs a more consistent focus on the question in an analytical, not descriptive, way. This paragraph is working at a low level 3.

Quality of Written Communication There are some grammatical mistakes in this paragraph. Some sentences contain several ideas and should have been split up. For example 'The acquisition of Texas brought about some problems later on, between slave and non-slave states, which led to the Civil War, but California brought about the gold rush of 1849' does not make clear the relationship of the acquisition of Texas to the 'problems' of the slave and non-slave states, and the relationship of these to the American Civil War. The comment about the Californian Gold Rush seems just added on, and the connection of this to the acquisition of Texas is not made.

The role of key individuals to inspire and motivate people to leave their settled homes in the east in favour of a move to the unknown and uncertain west was always going to be a tough yet uncertain job. President Polk was a huge believer in the western advancement, under his presidency more land was gained than under any other. Not only was he influential in expansion, but he helped spread the idealism of 'Manifest Destiny'. The belief that the white American could take any land they wanted as it was theirs for the taking, 'fierce national pride spurred the quest for land.'[20] This idea was used to justify wars and the oppressive treatment of the Indians. 'The Manifest Destiny became as sacrosanct as the constitution itself,'[21] that's how highly it was valued by the American people. Brigham Young was a key figure in the move of the Mormons from Illinois to Great Salt Lake Valley, in 1846 4000 of them led by Young made the journey westwards.[22] Their reasoning for movement was to escape religious persecution, Young thought the move to a new territory would do this and it did work, 'in the next two decades, recruitment boosted their number to more than 100 000'.[23] In the Salt Lake Valley they created their own infrastructures enabling them to settle completely in the west.

It was undoubtedly a combination of factors that led to the long-term settlement in the west, infrastructure however had the greatest significance of the time as the developments and advancements of it; made the west accessible to the people. The conflicts played their part in the acquiring of the land, but the desire and ability to move to these places needs to be instilled. The development of the transcontinental railroads made relocating and making a good life in the west easier. Goods and supplies could easily be exchanged, meaning people could make a decent living in the west. Government policy showed they had the intention of supporting the movement westwards but the policies only had limited success rates. The Homestead Act of 1862 for example did help encourage farmers to move West, but until 1873 when barbed wire was invented farming in the west was difficult with high rates of failure and had not been a family orientated style of farming, meaning long-term settlement was not going to happen. Settlement and expansion are two different things; each key in realising the dream of 'Manifest Destiny', but in settlement of people in the west infrastructural development was the most significant in the long-term continual settlement in the west. ☞

AO1 The student is here focusing on a third alternative factor: the role of individuals. However, this has not been considered as a factor, but rather as a way of describing the contribution made by two individuals: President Polk and Brigham Young. Far more individuals than just these two were involved. To achieve a higher level in the paragraph the student needs to consider the part played by individuals as a whole – as a factor to move change forward. Specific individuals should then be brought in as they provided examples of the way change was brought about. This paragraph is working at a low level 3.

Quality of Written Communication The student moves rapidly between different ideas, and the whole paragraph reads like a series of disconnected points. Some sentences should be split into two, for example in the second one there should be a break between 'advancement' and 'under'.

AO1 In this conclusion, the student is making a good attempt to pull all the strands together and reach a supported judgement. A distinction is made between factors that enabled the acquisition of land and factors that enabled the land to be settled, and a final judgement has been reached. However, a sharper focus on an analysis of the factors as drivers of change, rather than describing examples of each factor, would have made this conclusion stronger.

Endnotes

1. Jones, Maldwyn A., *The Limits of Liberty* (page 180)

2. Jones, Maldwyn A., *The Limits of Liberty* (page 180)

3. Murphy, D., Waldron M., Cooper, K., *United States 1740–1919*, 2008 (page 57)

4. Norton, Mary, *A People and a Nation*, 2007 (page 402)

5. Boyer, Paul, *The Enduring Vision: A History of the American People* (page 388)

6. Norton, Mary, *A People and a Nation*, 2007 (page 485)

7. Norton, Mary, *A People and a Nation*, 2007 (page 485)

8. Brogan, Hugh, *The Penguin History of the United States of America*, (page 256)

9. Norton, Mary, *A People and a Nation*, 2007 (page 244)

10. Jones, Maldwyn A., *The Limits of Liberty* (page 110)

11. Noy, Gary, *Distant Horizon: Documents from the nineteenth-century American West* (page 92)

12. Murphy, D., Waldron M., Cooper, K., *United States 1740–1919*, 2008 (page 57)

13. Socolofsky, Homer E., *Successes and Failures in Nebraska Homesteading*, 1968 (page 105)

14. Murphy, D., Waldron M., Cooper, K., *United States 1740–1919*, 2008 (page 57)

15. Jones, Maldwyn A., *The Limits of Liberty* (page 105)

16. Norton, Mary, *A People and a Nation*, 2007 (page 236)

17. Jones, Maldwyn A., *The Limits of Liberty* (page 105)

18. Boyer, Paul, *The Enduring Vision: A History of the American People*, (page 387)

19. Boyer, Paul, *The Enduring Vision: A History of the American People*, (page 387)

20. Norton, Mary, *A People and a Nation*, 2007 (page 297)

21. Jones, Maldwyn A., *The Limits of Liberty* (page 111)

22. Jones, Maldwyn A., *The Limits of Liberty* (page 178)

23. Boyer, Paul, *The Enduring Vision: A History of the American People*, (page 392)

The student has here used a wide range of different sources that are all appropriate for the enquiry. They have been referenced clearly. However, the endnotes should be consistent in the information they provide about sources used and should always include the publisher. ☞

AO1 The student has written a mainly analytical response with descriptive passages. The key issues have been teased out but rather than concentrating on them as issues, the student has put in a lot of descriptive material, writing about what happened and when, instead of focusing on the process of change. The inclusion of descriptive passages means that there is some drift from the focus of the question, which should always remain sharply focused on significance and change over time. In places the analysis lacks depth.

However the student has shown a clear understanding of the key issues involved, and has demonstrated a good understanding of the process of change over time. The main factors have been separated out with care and are directly related to change. There is a clear attempt to provide chronological balance, but this has not always been successful and there is a tendency for the main emphasis to be on change mid-century. A number of books and articles have been read, and have been used to support points made in the response.

The quality of communication does not match the quality of thought and understanding shown in the response. Sentences are too long and tend to be separated by commas and not full stops; expression is occasionally muddled and the very long paragraphs could be broken into shorter, more tightly focused ones.

Overall, this response is worthy of a **low level 3 for AO1 and would gain 16 out of 25 marks**.

Part B enquiry

To what extent can the role of the individual be considered the most important factor in the strengthening of the French monarchy, 1589–1715?

[25 marks]

This student is following the Edexcel-designed programme, CW9: *The Ascendancy of France 1589–1714.*

The enquiry title is appropriate for the coursework programme being followed and spans the entire timeframe of that programme. It focuses on change over time, using the 'role of individuals' as a factor to be compared with alternative factors in determining the most important in the process of change over time.

Grade A* student answer

France, in 1589–1715, came from being a struggling nation torn apart by religious war to being a dominant force within Europe, with an extremely powerful monarchy that could be considered absolute. It is debatable how far the strength of the monarchy was primarily enhanced by the role of the individual or whether other factors such as war and religion could be considered more important.

Henri IV's role in strengthening the French monarchy could be considered significant for a number of reasons, especially as he was able to stabilise France, which had to be the first step towards a strong Crown. He was a successful military leader, which enabled him to win victories over the Catholic League at Arques, Ivry and Fontaine-Française between 1589 and 1595.[1] It has also been said that 'the League won no great victories against him'.[2] Many deserted Henri initially because he was a Protestant, but military success is often a highly effective way to win loyalty and secure some power, thus showing the individual's character to be important in strengthening the French monarchy. Henri was also able to divide his enemies further when he converted to Catholicism in 1593, which left them with no objection to his rule even if they had their suspicions about his pragmatism. Henri also managed to end the religious wars for the time being with the Edict of Nantes, which allowed freedom of worship for the Huguenots but which also restricted their rights. Henri's ability to unite and stabilise France and therefore strengthen ☞

AO1 The student has written a brief introduction. Nevertheless, it conveys in a direct manner the focus of the enquiry: the dramatic change that took place in France between 1589 and 1715, and suggests what the factors that drove that change might have been.

AO1 The student has here written a clear analysis of the role of Henri IV in stabilising France and links this firmly to the strengthening of the French crown. The paragraph is focusing on Henri as a successful military leader, analysing throughout the significance of his success in uniting and stabilising France. Throughout, an explicit understanding is shown of the importance of this key issue.

the monarchy in such a way, shows the importance of Henri as an individual but also shows the importance of religion and his skill in recognising stability here as one of the keys to stability of the Crown.

Another important issue in securing France was restoring royal finances, which was left to the Duc de Sully who 'was able to transform this appalling state of finance'[3] and did manage to turn the Crown's debt of 200 000 million livres into a surplus of 15 000 000 livres, whilst still spending money to improve the French economy by setting up factories to reduce imports and improving the infrastructure for better trade and communications. This again shows the significant contribution of an individual in strengthening the Crown. However, as Alan James warns, 'Don't over-estimate Sully's achievements',[4] which despite the contrast with other interpretations may be a valid conclusion as many achievements, such as the surplus, did not outlive him and he had in many cases simply restructured debts rather than paying them off. It could be that Sully deliberately put policies in place that made him indispensable, and so protecting his career. This limits his contribution to the strengthening of the French Crown and perhaps limits the involvement of the role of the individual in changing events that are beyond his control.

After the regency of Louis XIII, Richelieu also needed to improve royal finances in order to strengthen the French Crown further. A particular problem was corruption, may have done something to reduce with the Elus, Crown financial representatives in some tax collecting districts, but which had not been solved completely. Richelieu created the Intendants whose loyalty to central government was greater than their loyalty to local authorities, and were moved around constantly so were unable to become too friendly with the local nobility. The parlements also became less autonomous where taxation was concerned by changing the regions that were Pays D'etat, areas in which local authorities could raise taxes, into Pays D'election, where the Crown could raise taxes. Richelieu has been credited as 'the principal architect of French absolutism',[5] whereas some historians believe that where finance was concerned his methods were 'fatally weakening'.[6] Whilst that might be true, it must be remembered that the system did manage to survive even times of heavy taxation. Based on the other concerns of the French monarchy at the time, such as Hapsburg encirclement, it may be fair to conclude that ☞

AO1 A sound analysis of the role of Sully, with an evaluation of his significance and the use of a secondary source to help focus on a judgement about his role. The footnoting used by the student is clear. However, whilst the use of websites to access material is acceptable, the material itself should be footnoted and not just the website.

AO1 A sound analysis of the significance of the role of Richelieu in strengthening the French monarchy by bringing about necessary change. Reference is made to wider reading in support for judgements made in respect of the debate about Richelieu's effectiveness. The student has shown the ability to stand back from what they have read and absorb it into their argument.

Richelieu 'couldn't have done much better',[7] so was as successful as he could have been in strengthening the French Crown. Richelieu, though not particularly religious, could not tolerate the Huguenots as an independent military force, perceiving this as threatening the Crown's absolutism. He was able to subdue them at La Rochelle, destroying the Huguenots as a military force but allowing their worship to continue. These successes show Richelieu's importance as an individual, strengthening the monarchy and completing a task that others had failed to do in the past. They also show his understanding of the importance of controlling military forces indicative of the significance of military strength and conflict for a strong monarchy, as well as balancing this with the maintenance of religious tolerance.

After Richelieu's death, and especially after Louis XIII's death, Cardinal Mazarin became the first minister of France and largely continues Richelieu's policies with the same aims and ambitions. It has been said that Mazarin's policies 'lacked the strength of Richelieu's'[8] and it is certainly true that he wasn't as effective at using propaganda. However, that is not to say there were no positive achievements, which is why it could be said that he was 'arguably a pivotal figure'.[9] The power of Intendants had been reduced in the past years and Mazarin re-established their role, allowing central government to regain greater control over taxation in the provinces. Mazarin also continued Richelieu's policy of war and, although expensive, he was able to gain a favourable settlement for France in the Treaty of Westphalia. This increased the power of the French Crown through enhanced prestige and the lessening of the threat of invasion, showing that Mazarin, by following Richelieu's policies, proved to be an effective individual in strengthening the French monarchy and therefore further emphasising the importance of the role of the individual. Interestingly, Mazarin advised the young Louis XIV that it would be best if he became his own first minister. Although the motives behind this advice may have been many, it did possibly lead to Louis XIV becoming very involved in the governance of France enabling him to become an absolute monarch.

Another key individual from the reign of Louis XIV was Jean-Baptiste Colbert, who dominated finance and it is generally believed that he was a success. 'Under the guidance of Colbert, the French economy did well'.[10] He believed in mercantilism, the theory that a ☞

AO1 The student is here giving a clear and detailed analysis of the role of Mazarin in strengthening the French monarchy, linking back to the work of Richelieu and forward to the advice given by Mazarin to the young monarch Louis XIV. By referencing the views of historians (by endnotes) the student is showing an excellent awareness of the debate about the part played by Mazarin.

AO1 A sound analysis of the part Colbert played in introducing mercantilism, with a clear focus on the role of individuals. The paragraph shows a clear understanding of the significance of the theory and of the system of mercantilism. This is firmly linked to the enquiry focus and demonstrates a detailed understanding of the process of change.

country's power was represented by its capital and that to increase this power it should maximise exports and minimise imports. He made improvements to the economy and increased the power of the French Crown by setting up trading companies, attempting to bring private activity under the authority of the state with policies such as the Code de la Draperie. The Controle General also supervised subordinate organisations bringing finance under one central method of control. These policies increased trade and government involvement, and therefore the power of the Crown, as the state was more directly involved, showing Colbert to have made a significant contribution as an individual, promoting mercantilism.

Louis XIV also played a significant part in government. Most business was conduced at Versailles, a centre of power where all policy was deployed by the King. He also frequently met with his conseil d'en haut, which was small, consisting of about five loyal and able men rather than the nobility. This kind of council made business more efficient; his councillors were therefore effective and the power of the nobility over the government was limited. Louis' methods thus increased the power of the monarchy through his personal involvement, showing, again, the importance of the role of the individual.

AO1 The student is here placing a strong emphasis on the role of Louis XIV in strengthening the monarchy by his involvement in policy-making and delivery, and by working with a tight circle of able advisers that were not necessarily of the nobility.

It could be argued that war and conflict played an important part also. Henri IV may not have been as successful in securing the throne had he not had the military ability to fight the Catholic League and inspire his followers. The ability to fight a war effectively was an important part in the strengthening of France. Also, although Henri wanted to avoid joining a war that would adversely affect France, he declared war on Spain in 1595, which created anti-Spanish feeling in France, giving a common enemy to French Catholics and Protestants and thus helping to strengthen the monarchy by giving the two religions reason to unite.

AO1 In this paragraph the student is moving to a consideration of an alternative factor to that of individuals. The importance of war and conflict is analysed, showing an excellent understanding of the significance of the factor and of the part it played in strengthening the monarchy under Henri IV.

France also gained from the Thirty Years' War, making territorial gains and winning an edge over Europe with Hapsburg power diminished and France's glory and reputation enhanced. Whilst this probably benefited the security and wealth of the monarchy as such, it may also have done more for the power of France within Europe. It should be appreciated that the monarchy may have suffered as a result of the heavy taxation needed to fund the war, thus temporarily damaging the ☞

AO1 The student here is developing an understanding of the importance of war and conflict by focusing on the importance of the Thirty Years' War and analysing its significance in strengthening France and the French monarchy. Whilst appreciating that this significance was not always positive, the student turns this to good effect by showing that war generated a strong army and navy which kept France peaceful at home and safeguarded French overseas trade. This is a sound analysis that directly explores the process of change.

economy, reducing the power of the Intendants and risking rebellion. However, despite these problems, the monarchy did survive and war required an expansion of the army, which protected France and made it easier to keep subjects in order, and the navy, which kept French seaways safe thus improving trade. So war had outcomes that were directly beneficial to the French monarchy, showing it to be an important factor in strengthening the Crown, although not always entirely successful.

Mazarin's continuation of foreign wars allowed France to benefit from the Treaty of Westphalia, but also may have led to the Frondes through unpopular taxation. The Frondes represent another conflict, which could be seen to lead to a more absolute monarchy. Although not benefiting the state initially, the Frondes failed due to the mistakes of the Frondeurs, and showed a lack of strength in the opposition to the government. They had a considerable effect on Louis XIV who never forgot the Frondes and was influenced by them to always keep nobles in their place and never fully trusting them. Conflict thus led to a successful policy for the French Crown, enhancing its power. Indeed, James concludes the Frondes were 'a springboard for the illustrious reign that followed.'[11]

AO1 The student here returns to the role of Mazarin, but this time in the context of his continuation of foreign wars. This further develops the analysis of the role of individuals and connects it strongly with the analysis of an alternative factor, that of war and conflict. Throughout, the student remains focused on the strengthening of the French monarchy.

Louis XIV loved to engage in war and pursue *Gloire*. In some cases, there was the possibility of going to war to avoid encirclement, but most ventures were the result of political rivalry. It is arguable how far they could benefit the French monarchy any more than by enhancing its reputation. Whilst foreign policy allowed Louis to make some gains, such as Strasburg in 1681 and Luxemburg 1684, Norman H. Davies states: 'France's ambitions were trimmed'[12] and 'the Dutch, like the French, were exhausted,'[13] showing that war over the Spanish Succession may have been costly with few gains and ambitions lessened due to the outcomes. Like most nations at war, there was also a huge amount of debt, with an income of 69 million livres and expenditure higher, at about 132 million livres.[14] War towards the end of the time period may have, indeed, damaged the French monarchy overall, perhaps suggesting war to be a less important factor in strengthening the Crown during this period.

AO1 The student is here considering a factor – war – as an alternative to the 'role of the individual' in bringing about change to the French monarchy. The student has written a developed and sustained analysis of the role of war in strengthening the French monarchy 1589–1715, which also takes account of the pace of change. Judgements made are effectively backed by reference to appropriate secondary source material.

Religion also played a part. France was largely a Catholic country when the Protestant Henri IV became king, but his conversion to Catholicism allowed him to split the Catholic League and so remove a key reason for ☞

opposition to the Crown, showing how religion can be used to greatly increase the security and strength of the monarch. The Edict of Nantes ended religious wars for the time being, demonstrating how religious issues played a large part in restoring stability. However, this also created a 'state within a state'[15] as Huguenots had secure towns, so thus in dealing with religion in one way another problem was created for the monarchy, thus reducing its importance as a vehicle for change. During the Thirty Years' War, the importance of religion was also qualified. Richelieu allied France with German Protestant nations, which proved successful in challenging Spain and the Hapsburgs 'when Richelieu's German allies presented him with a fortress…French fortunes were mounting.'[16] However, subduing the Huguenot military force was a significant achievement showing the importance of controlling religion in a country if the monarchy is to be strong. Louis XIV's religious policy originally strengthened his power by forming a Gallican Church filled with relatives of ministers who were loyal to him and passing the Declaration of the Four Articles, limiting the Pope's authority in Church matters. However, after his second marriage his attitude to, and policy relating to, religious matters changed dramatically; influenced by the Jesuits he revoked the Edict of Nantes in 1685. By then, Louis probably considered himself strong enough not to have to worry about Protestant rebellion and so strengthened the French monarchy, with all subjects conforming to the faith of the King, making the monarchy even more secure in its absolutism.

In conclusion, the role of the individual was definitely a key factor in strengthening the French monarchy 1589–1715. Some important reasons the monarchy was able to grow in power was the military and political skill of Henri IV, making him able to strengthen and stabilise France; moves towards central government having more control initiated by Richelieu and continued by Mazarin; the personal government of Louis XIV, and improved finances due to the work of Sully and Colbert. These relate to the success of individuals and highlight the importance of able rulers and ministers. However, war and conflict is also an important factor as it led to an improved military force, which increases the ruler's power, and the Frondes induced Louis XIV to prevent nobles becoming too powerful. However, since war created several internal problems, such as near economic collapse, it may not have been as important in strengthening the ☞

AO1 The student here gives a sustained and developed analysis of the role of religion in strengthening the French monarchy, and weaves it back through the Thirty Years' War, Richelieu and the policies of Louis XIV, effectively analysing its role in strengthening the French monarchy. The candidate is showing a sound understanding of the process of change over time. The analysis is well supported by an appropriate range of factual sources.

AO1 The student has written a strong conclusion. The immediate focus is on the presented factor – the role of the individuals. The reasons given for the judgement that this is the key factor are given succinctly and clearly. Two other factors that have been considered in detail in the main body of the response are war and conflict, and religion. Here, their role in bringing about change is summarised and a clear judgement reached as to why they were not the key factors in bringing about change. The final sentence pulls this together soundly.

French monarchy as the role of the individual. Though religion is often secondary to traditional rivalry in foreign conflict, the effectiveness of Henri IV's abjuration, quelling Huguenots as a military force and bringing all of France under the religion of the king, should be kept in mind. Overall, the role of the individual seems to be the most important single factor, but was much more effective when war and conflict was used to improve French fortune and religious issues were effectively controlled.

Endnotes

1. Internet resource, University of Leicester

2. ibid

3. Murphy, Derrick, Tillbrook Michael & Walsh-Atkins, Patrick, *Europe 1450–1661*, Collins Educational, 2000

4. James, Alan, *The Origins of French Absolutism 1598–1661*, Pearson Longman, 2006

5. ibid

6. Murphy, Derrick, Tillbrook Michael & Walsh-Atkins, Patrick, *Europe 1450–1661*, Collins Educational, 2000

7. James, Alan, *The Origins of French Absolutism 1598–1661*, Pearson Longman, 2006

8. Internet resource

9. Wilkinson, Richard, *Louis XIV*, Routledge, 2007

10. Internet resource

11. James, Alan, *The Origins of French Absolutism 1598–1661*, Pearson Longman, 2006

12. Davies, Norman H., *Europe: A History*, Pimlico, 2007

13. ibid

14. ibid

15. Murphy, Derrick, Tillbrook Michael & Walsh-Atkins, Patrick, *Europe 1450–1661*, Collins Educational 2000

16. Davies, Norman H., *Europe: A History*, Pimlico 2007

The student has clearly used a good range of source material, providing evidence of wide reading. The only problem with these endnotes is that there are four references to the internet, but no indication is given as to what was seen, read and noted. Using the internet as a resource is perfectly acceptable, but the actual material accessed must be referenced.

The student has written a sustained analysis, which directly explores the process of change over the period, providing chronological balance. In electing to analyse the role of individuals as a factor to be compared with alternative factors in bringing about change to the strength of the French monarchy, they have identified a number of key individuals and analysed their contribution. The student here has avoided the temptation to write mini-biographies of selected individuals, but it is very tempting to do this if the approach here is adopted. An alternative, and possibly better, approach would have been to construct the argument for the importance of the role of individuals, bringing in specific people as they exemplified specific points being made. The student has demonstrated a clear understanding of the key issues raised by the enquiry and has evaluated various points made by the sources consulted. A range of appropriate sources spanning the period has been consulted and used with discrimination in reaching considered judgements.

Despite occasional grammatical mistakes, the response is generally clear and lucid.

Overall, this response is worthy of a **high level 5 for AO1 and would gain 24/25 marks**.

Complete assignment for *CW42: The Making of Modern China c1900–2000*

Each coursework assignment is, as you know, made up of a Part A enquiry focusing on short-term significance and a Part B enquiry focusing on change over a period of not less than 100 years. You have just read through two Part A enquiries and two Part B enquiries scoring marks at C and A*. Now read through the complete enquiry that follows (for the Edexcel-designed coursework programme *CW42: The Making of Modern China c1900–2000),* with both parts scoring at A*.

Part A enquiry

What was the short-term significance of the Tiananmen Square massacre of 1989?

[25 marks]

The student is following the Edexcel-designed coursework programme *CW42: The Making of Modern China c1900–2000.* The focus of the programme is on 'the political, social and economic transformation of China in the 20th century and the factors influential in this process'. The contemporary sources have not been reproduced in this book.

This is a valid historical question and relates well to the short-term significance of an event that is of direct relevance to the coursework programme.

The student has used five contemporary sources, and has referred to them by number in the response.

1. Interview at Tiananmen Square with Chai Ling

2. Adie, Kate, 'Kate Adie returns to Tiananmen Square', broadcast 3 June 2009

3. Richelson, Jeffry T. and Michael L. Evans, *National Security Archive Electronic Briefing Book No 16,* 1 June 1999

7. Becker, Jasper and Gittings, John, article in *The Guardian,* 5 June 1989

11. Excerpts from Party Central Office Secretariat Minutes of the CCP Central Politburo Standing Committee Meeting, 6 June 1989

The secondary sources used were provided in endnotes.

The student has identified sources that together provide both range and depth, enabling the enquiry to be appropriately researched. The footnoting of secondary sources used is clear.

Grade A* student answer

The short-term significance of an event is best defined as the impact it had over a period spanning from immediately following the event up until twenty years later. It is undeniable that the Tiananmen Square massacre of 1989 was greatly significant, and its impact can still be seen in today's China. The event revealed divisions within the Chinese Communist Party with the resurgence of hardliners and Deng's political manoeuvring, as implied in a number of contemporary accounts such as excerpts from a CCP meeting and Kate Adie's documentary. This source also raises another important outcome of the event: the sacrifice of political freedom to ☞

This is an excellent opening paragraph. The student defines what is meant by 'short-term significance', outlines the key issues and indicates the way in which the contemporary and secondary source material is going to be used. An indication of the likely main conclusion is given. However, the sentence focusing just on Source 11 is an unnecessary distracter at this stage and the introduction would work better if it were omitted.

safeguard the continuation of economic reform, which is also supported by historians Fenby and Gittings. Whilst many sources support the view that China's economy boomed from the nineties onwards, others consider the economic impact caused by international condemnation of the massacre, which strained China's foreign relations. Perhaps the most significant outcome of Tiananmen, however, was that it ended the democracy movement in China and therefore secured the continuation of the CCP's rule.

The Tiananmen Square protests caused instability and divisions within the politburo. Source 2 describes there to have been a 'vicious power struggle' between the 'old guard' and 'liberal voices sympathetic to the calls for reform.' It also focuses on the dominance of hardliners within the party: 'Bao Tung … resigned from the party in protest. He was immediately arrested and accused of spreading counter-revolutionary propaganda.' This shows how party members, such as Bao Tung, who were sympathetic to the students' cause, suffered at the hands of those who were not. Source 11 also illustrates this through the simple fact that Zhao Ziyang was not present, having been replaced by the incoming General Secretary Jiang. The source also presents divisions within the CCP: 'It's going to take a lot of work to get order restored.' This opinion, offered by Qiao Shi, who also claimed that innocent 'onlookers' were killed, contrasts sharply with some of the other leaders, who maintained that 'putting down the riots' would restore social order, and that 'no one was killed within Tiananmen Square'. This source is comprised of excerpts from a CCP meeting two days subsequent to the event. It therefore provides an accurate insight into the workings of the Party and demonstrates clearly the disagreements that arose. Whilst it could be argued that Source 2 may portray a potentially over-critical Western view, the fact that its content agrees with Source 11 gives Kate Adie's documentary credibility. Fenby argues that whilst the leaders collectively knew that dialogue would be ineffective, there was division among them as to whether government measures should take a 'soft form, as favoured by Zhao', or 'entrenched hard-line power'[1] would advocate supremely tough measures. Ultimately, as Source 11 shows, the hardliners triumphed: 'The key to stabilising things right now is to be super tough in tracking down the counter-revolutionary rioters.' Source 3 further illustrates instability within the party: 'the leadership crisis'. Whilst perhaps this assessment is inaccurate, as the West could not have known the ☞

AO1 An analytical response that relates directly to the main focus of the question. It focuses confidently on the significance of one outcome of the massacre: the instability and divisions within the *Politburo*. It shows a clear understanding of the centrality of this key issue.

AO2 The evidence is interrogated confidently and critically in order to identify issues and make and support judgements. It is well-related to its historical context. The student here is making some detailed cross-referencing between Sources 2 and 11, showing how the splits within the CCP were reflected in, and supported by, Source 11. This is further supported by reference to the work of historian Jonathan Fenby. In making the cross-referencing, the reliability of both contemporary sources is considered. Further cross-referencing to Source 3 confirms instability within the party, which is further confirmed by the work of Jonathan Spence.

situation within the politburo at the time for certain, Spence qualifies it, depicting how 'Deng Xiaoping's position...had been seriously weakened by the events of 1989.'[2]

A significant outcome of the Tiananmen Square massacre was, as put by Source 11, the tightening of political control 'for the sake of reform and opening and modern construction'. Source 2 also implies this, describing the 'unspoken agreement that you can get rich while the party makes the decisions'. Furthermore, Kate Adie depicts the colossal economic progress following 1989: 'in the last two decades China has throbbed with economic progress ... 270000 have been dragged out of medieval poverty.' In terms of provenance, the documentary contains footage from 1989 and the present day, allowing clear comparison between the two periods in terms of economic development, thus qualifying her statements. Source 1, however, depicts the protestors as 'striving for rights' and that if political freedom was not achieved, China would 'retreat into another dark age.' Yet this source is an interview with Chai Ling. Being a prominent student leader during the protests, her response could be seen as a mere exaggeration in order to gain sympathy for the student cause. The source also dates from 1989 and therefore lacks credibility in terms of analysing the effect of the Massacre on China's future. In fact, other contemporary accounts largely suggest that the staggering economic growth and prosperity following 1989 has vindicated the lack of political freedom. Whilst Source 1 suggests that the repression of democracy would endanger China's future, Source 3 connotes the contrary: 'if the way we handled the Tiananmen crisis was incorrect, we would not have today's prosperity.' This source must be taken with caution, as it originates from the president of a Chinese government's think tank, therefore possibly being biased in the interests of the CCP and potential propaganda. Nevertheless, it raises a significant point: that the suppression of the movement enabled economic reforms to proceed. Gittings highlights Deng's belief that 'the modernisation process on a backward country needs strong-arm politics with authority, rather than Western-style democracy as a driving force.'[3] Fenby confirms this assessment: 'The crushing of dissent in 1989 marked a fundamental choice by the Chinese leadership which endured into the 21st century.'[4] This solidifies the view that China faced a trade-off between political ☞

AO1 The student here explores the key issue of the relationship between the crushing of political dissent and economic prosperity. Whilst the secondary sources used are all appropriate as sources of information, some analysis based on the student's own knowledge and understanding would have raised the mark within the level.

AO2 The student is here interrogating the sources critically and with confidence and using some effective cross-referencing in order to establish the relationship between the repression of political dissenters as a result of the Tiananmen Square Massacre and the growth of the economy. Historians Gittings and Fenby are used to support the judgement made – that political dissent was the price that had to be paid for economic revival.

freedom and economic prosperity, and the results of Tiananmen allowed such developments to occur.

Despite China's economic prosperity seen today, this was not always the case due to sanctions imposed following the Massacre, and at the time international condemnation made China's future seem uncertain. Source 11 suggests that China's domestic situation was dire: 'losses of thirty to forty million yuan every day.' Source 3 takes this further, exemplifying how international condemnation exacerbated the problem: 'President Bush announced a package of sanctions against the PRC.' This included the suspension of weapon sales and the additional suspension of World Bank loans. Source 7 seems to agree with Source 3: 'President Bush denounced China for using military force against the demonstrators; Mrs Thatcher said that Britain was "appalled at the indiscriminate shooting of unarmed people".' This suggests there was heavy international criticism following the massacre. Source 7 is an article from the *Guardian*, a British broadsheet newspaper, dated 7 June 1989. Consequently it can be inferred that it would accurately portray the West's interpretation of the event. Furthermore, as John Gittings, a well-respected historian, was present on 4 June, descriptions of the event as a 'bloody spectacle' are likely to be accurate and not politically influenced, as he would appreciate the value of objectivity. Similarly, Source 3 contains documents describing information passed between Washington DC and the US embassy in Beijing. This would also suggest it reliably portrays the western take on the event. Gittings supports the view that foreign condemnation exacerbated China's problems, stating that 'the loss of foreign investment in 1989 was estimated at one to two billion US dollars, while tourism fell by one billion.'[5] Source 1 suggests the harsh extent of foreign condemnation: 'All the Western countries … are issuing one or another kind of proclamation about applying sanctions against China and cutting China off from the world.' However, Source 3 does not support this accusation, expressing America's wish to 'keep open the lines of communication … and assure a healthy relationship.' This would certainly seem a more reliable representation of the Western countries as the source originates from the US and not the CCP. Fenby qualifies this, stating that 'no nation broke off diplomatic relations'[6] and in 2008 China hosted the Olympics, which indicates it has risen in international status and had a powerful global presence. It is therefore arguable that sanctions and condemnation were only significant ☞

AO1 This is an excellent analytical paragraph relating well to the focus of the enquiry by showing a clear understanding of the impact international condemnation had on China's immediate economic prosperity. The analysis is supported by well-selected factual material that is completely relevant.

AO2 The issue (that of the impact of the Massacre on the outside world) is clearly identified and relevant contemporary sources are used to develop this. The contemporary sources are interpreted and evaluated in order to determine the attitudes of the West, and extracts from appropriate secondary sources are used to support or challenge the conclusions that are reached. There is some excellent cross-referencing for reliability and credibility.

The evidence arising from an evaluation of the contemporary sources has been carefully considered in order to determine the weight that should be given to each source when reaching a judgement.

in the immediate aftermath of Tiananmen, in the very short term, and did not have such a profound impact as others.

Finally, the suppression of the protest ensured the CCP's survival. Source 2 summarised Tiananmen as a 'protest that ended in bloodshed'. This signified, most importantly, the end of the democracy movement in China. Source 7 also portrays this: 'armoured vehicles pushed over and crushed the plaster replica of the Statue of Liberty, which had become a symbol of the students' hopes of a democratic revolution.' The crushing of the 'Goddess of Democracy' symbolised the CCP's victory over the people. Chai Ling suggests how the student protests were a futile attempt at establishing democracy: 'there are certain people and certain events in history that are destined to fail.' Source 2 supports this view, concluding that 'China would never have western-style multiparty elections.' It also suggests how 1989 highlighted the backwardness of the CCP rule: 'do they understand what kind of a world they are in now?' This connotes how the party was out-dated in a world where communism was falling in favour of less repressive democratic institutions. Gittings maintains this view, arguing that the Tiananmen Square massacre of 1989 was the clearest possible indication that 'the Chinese Communist Party had lost its mandate.'[7] Source 11 represents the CCP's belief that the suppression of protest was necessary, otherwise 'we'd have civil war'. Whilst Zhu Mizhi's motive is dubious, he also supports the view in Source 3: 'China would be in chaos. The people would have risen and resisted the government.' What does potentially add weight to his assessment is the fact that the source originated ten years after the crackdown and so since the Chinese government is still in control and civil war had not occurred, it can be assumed that the suppression of the protest was justified in ensuring stability. Fenby illustrates this also, by stating that the Tiananmen Square massacre was classified as a 'necessary ingredient'[8] in maintaining stability. Furthermore, if China's past is considered, then the one-party state and repression of political freedom are reasonable as, when this has not been the case in the past, China has been rife with political instability as in the Warlord Era. Ultimately, Spence validates this short-term significance: '... would be able to hold onto its power and prerequisites ... through a delicate balancing act of selectively stifling domestic criticism and dissent.'[9] This explicitly demonstrates how the suppression of the protests secured the continuation of the CCP's monopoly power. ☞

AO1 The survival of the CCP is the issue being addressed here. The student demonstrates an excellent understanding of the impact of the Massacre on this issue and discusses the implications of the attempted, and to a very large extent, successful suppression of democracy. The paragraph is wholly analytical and supported by well-selected factual material.

AO2 The student is here working with a good range of source material, which is interrogated well and the evidence so derived is evaluated. The sources are effectively cross-referenced and evaluated within the context of the values of the time. Support for the evaluation is found in an appropriate selection of arguments from the secondary sources.

In conclusion, it is clear that the short-term significance of the Tiananmen Square Massacre in 1989 was to ensure political stability with the continuation of CCP rule. Ultimately, this was the most important, due to its very close link to the staggering economic progress made after 1989. This is because the lack of political freedom, in other words, the dictatorship of the CCP, ensured that Deng's plans for economic reform went ahead. It could be argued that the dominance of hardliners within the Party aided this, as it certainly enabled the continuation of CCP supremacy. On the other hand, it is unknown whether taking a softer approach would have achieved the same results, and, in fact, may not have led to such a massacre. Furthermore, although international condemnation and the subsequent imposition of sanctions hindered China's economic development, it did not last for more than a few years. This suggests it to be less significant in comparison to other outcomes of the Tiananmen Square massacre. Nevertheless, in the short term it lasted, it did serve as a warning to China's future. On balance, all the sources depict different reasons for the short-term significance of the event, but overall, what is inherent throughout all of them, whether implicitly or explicitly, is the suppression of the Tiananmen Square protest and the maintenance of CCP monopoly rule for many years to come.

An excellent conclusion, drawing together all the strands of argument pointing to the key issues that emerged from the Tiananmen Square massacre. The student shows a clear and competent understanding of the issues themselves, and of the ways in which they relate to each other. The evidence derived from the sources is integrated into the conclusion and a sound and supported judgement reached.

Endnotes

1. Fenby, Jonathan, *The Penguin History of Modern China*, 2009 (page 590)

2. Spence, Jonathan D., *The Search for Modern China*, 1999 (page 707)

3. Gittings, John, *The Changing Face of China from Mao to Market*, 2006 (page 225)

4. Fenby, Jonathan, *The Penguin History of Modern China*, 2009 (page 639)

5. Gittings, John, *The Changing Face of China from Mao to Market*, 2006 (page 248)

6. Fenby, Jonathan, *The Penguin History of Modern China*, 2009 (page 631)

7. Gittings, John, *The Changing Face of China from Mao to Market*, 2006 (page 246)

8. Fenby, Jonathan, *The Penguin History of Modern China*, 2009 (page 678)

9. Spence, Jonathan D., *The Search for Modern China*, 1999 (page 708)

The student has used three secondary sources throughout the response. They are all relevant and, because they are written by modern historians, have up-to-date views regarding the development of China in the 20th century. Extracts from the three books have been used well in challenge and support of judgements reached from an evaluation of the contemporary sources. ☞

AO1 The student has been working at a high level 4 throughout.

The response is analytical throughout, and relates well to the focus of the question. There is a confident focus on the short-term significance of the Tiananmen Square Massacre, and the major key issues are clearly identified. The analysis is supported by well-selected factual material that is wholly relevant and well balanced. However, the student's own understanding of the historical context was sometimes implicit rather than explicit.

The discussion is controlled and balanced, and the results of the enquiry presented in a logical way. There are no grammatical errors and the student uses an extensive range of vocabulary.

Overall, this response is worthy of a **high level 4 for AO1 and would gain 12/13 marks**.

AO2 The student has been working within level 4 throughout. The question is thoroughly investigated; a wide range of appropriate sources has been selected and their evidence integrated into a structured and sustained argument. In so doing, the status of the evidence is considered. There is confident interrogation of the source material and the evidence so derived used critically to raise and analyse the key issues. There is an understanding of the need to explore the implications of the evidence in the light of its historical context and the values of the society from which it comes.

QoWC The quality of written communication matches the quality of the historical understanding shown.

Overall, this response is worthy of a **high level 4 for AO2 and would gain the full 12 marks**.

Part B enquiry

How far can the establishment of the People's Republic of China in 1949 be considered as the key turning point in the development of China, 1900–2000?

[25 marks]

An appropriate, clearly expressed, enquiry title. A turning point approach has been selected, which means that the student will be looking for patterns of change across the century.

Grade A* student answer

In 1900, China was a weak, out-dated imperial nation in a state of decline. One hundred years later, a rather different China existed, having been transformed into a rising global super power with a strong government and economy, and a generally healthy, literate and prospering population. This colossal difference suggests there to have been major development in terms of economic, political, social and cultural change and progression of events. A turning point is definable as an event that brings about a historical change upon which important developments hinge. In this sense it is clear that the establishment of the People's Republic of China can be considered as a turning point as it marked the beginning of communist rule in China and resulted in a number of significant changes to China's culture, society and, to a lesser extent, economy. However, the 1919 May Fourth Movement and the 1978 Third Plenum must also be considered; the former essentially bringing about a shift in social and cultural ideology which had a significant impact on China's development, and the latter having a profound impact on Chinese economics, which caused enormous change, perhaps being the key turning point. By examining the key themes mentioned above, this essay will attempt to establish which of these events can be considered as the key turning point of the 20th century.

The May Fourth Movement was the greatest display of national feeling that China had ever seen at the time. The event transformed national politics, with demonstrations, boycotts and strikes by a wide cross-section of society, from students and intellectuals to businessmen ☞

An excellent introduction. In the first two sentences, the student sets out the nature of the problem upon which the enquiry will be focused, which is the huge contrast between China in 1900 and China in 2000. The student shows an awareness that this will involve a consideration of economic, political, social and cultural change. The student then gives a definition of a turning point, which is the approach that will be taken. The presented turning point is the 'establishment of the People's Republic of China', and two more will be addressed (the 1919 May Fourth movement and the 1978 Third Plenum) and in this way chronological balance should be achieved.

AO1 The student here focuses on the May Fourth Movement, which is appropriately contextualised. However, the focus on the Movement as a turning point is more implicit than explicit. The student does, however, have a clear understanding as to what changed as a result and what stayed the same. The paragraph is analytical and supported by accurate factual material.

and workers. It marked the turning of a generation towards political activism and student rebellion established itself as a means of communicating their beliefs and ideas; supported by the frequency of student uprisings in subsequent decades, for example, the May Thirtieth Movement. Furthermore, it not only revived the nationalist movement, but also led to the birth of the CCP in 1921, introducing communism into China. However, whilst the people successfully prevented the government from signing the treaty, the movement in fact brought no change to China's political structure, as a real democratic system was not established.

Whilst the founding of the Chinese Communist Party (attributed to the May Fourth Movement) was undeniably a change in Chinese politics, what was more significant was the change 1949 resulted in: the dominance of communist ideology and rule in China. Mao claimed the new system as being 'under the leadership of the working class',[1] indicating a break from the elitist system that both the Manchus and Guo Min Dang ruled by. Moreover, following the dissolution of the Qing dynasty was an unstable period, ranging from warlord rule to numerous wars. The establishment of the People's Republic of China denoted the end of this political volatility. The CCP had successfully accomplished the reintegration of China that previous leaders had failed to do as the People's Liberation Army allowed it to extend its control and unify the country under one leader. Also, Mao proclaimed that 'China has stood up',[2] signifying the end of foreign dominance over China. An example being Yuan Shikai succumbing to Japan's 'Twenty-One Demands', compared to the CCP regaining Chinese land occupied by Japan such as Manchuria. However, significant continuity prevailed, despite ideological change. Many party cadres found themselves subordinate to the 'class enemies' they thought, under communism, they were going to oust. Furthermore, the political structure of CCP rule closely resembled that of Chiang Kai-Shek and the monarchy beforehand, suggesting little actual change.

The Third Plenum brought about mild political change. The party shifted its authority 'from the leadership to lower levels'[3] and government injunction no longer ran everywhere. International relations had also developed under Deng. In 1997 Britain peacefully restored Hong Kong to the Chinese, as did the Portuguese with Macao in 1999. Moreover, Deng's visit to President Carter ☞

AO1 This is a sustained analysis of the potential of the founding of the PRC to be a key turning point. An excellent understanding of the context of the turning point is shown. Links with the May Fourth Movement and the CCP are effectively made and analysed. Support is given by carefully-selected secondary source material, and there is throughout a sustained exploration of political change and continuity.

in 1979 was far the more successful compared to Nixon's visit with Mao in 1972. This signifies considerable change from China's traditional xenophobic attitude. During the Plenum, Hua Guofeng was forced to self-criticise for adhering to the 'Two Whatevers',[4] exemplifying Deng's break from Maoism, as under Deng's leadership the cult of Mao largely disappeared and criticism of the 'Great Leader' became commonplace. Nevertheless, political change was limited. In fact, the party continued to regard Mao with reverence: 'His immense contributions are immortal.'[5] Furthermore, Deng firmly believed in Marxism-Leninism, suggested by his rejection of the 'fifth modernisation'. Also, the 'four great freedoms' were removed from the constitution following the suppression of the 1979 Democracy Wall Movement, illustrating continuity as it reinforced oppressive Chinese customs. The Tiananmen Square Massacre not only depicts this, but also the brutal response of government-paralleled violence imposed by preceding administrations, for example, during the Cultural Revolution.

Evidence would suggest that in fact the establishment of the People's Republic of China was the key political turning point as it brought about the greatest political change. May Fourth achieved no real result, and the Third Plenum largely built upon previous communist policies.

The establishment of the PRC created limited economic change, perhaps the most notable being its ability to reduce inflation from 1000% to 15% by 1951.[6] This marked a significant change from the rapidly increasing inflation that effectively destroyed Chiang Kai-Shek's government, but also contrasts with the creeping insurgence of inflation under Deng and onwards. During 1958–78 the PRC created a rural apparatus that no previous government had ever envisaged,[7] bringing great economic benefits to the countryside. Coupled with unprecedented land reform policies, this opened the possibility for poor peasants to survive, unlike before. Also, further economic changes accompanying communism were the state ownership of both the agricultural and industrial sectors, and collectivisation. Furthermore, the first Five Year Plan led to huge GDP growth and a rise in agricultural output greater in relation to population increase. However, when comparing these results with previous output levels it becomes apparent that, although the CCP introduced different economic policies, the outcome barely differed from before. For example, between 1912 and 1933, ☞

AO1 This paragraph shows a strong analysis of political change and continuity resulting from the Third Plenum. The student has demonstrated a clear understanding of its function within the context of this enquiry. Relevant extracts from secondary sources are chosen to support the argument that the Third Plenum brought about only mild political change.

AO1 The student has returned to a consideration of the PRC as a key turning point, and is working at level 5 in this sustained analysis of the establishment of the PRC as a key turning point. The previous paragraphs had focused on political change and continuity, and here the student's attention is focused on an excellent analysis of economic change and continuity. Evidence is provided in support of points made.

Yet, by making the relationship between the PRC and the CCP more explicit, the student could have further improved the paragraph.

China's GDP grew from CH$113 to CH$123 and the annual rate of growth was over 6%.[8] Plus, the marketed agricultural surplus had increased by about 50%,[9] despite the population rise.

The Third Plenum laid out requirements of the Four Modernisations, marking the beginning of the reform era. The saying, 'It doesn't matter if a cat is black or white; if it can catch mice, it's a good cat,'[10] demonstrates Deng's shift towards pragmatic economic policy from ideological. Deng deviated from centralised control of the economy, collectivisation and material-balance planning, also refusing to carry out Hua's Ten-Year Plan, proving his abandonment of Marxist political economy and signifying great change in Chinese communism.[11] Forced treaty ports and trade concessions were common in the early 20th century and widely resented amongst the populace. However, Deng's Open Door policy and establishment of four Special Economic Zones in 1979 opened Chinese markets to foreign trade and investment, suggesting a change in international economic policy. Moreover, Deng initiated the reversal of sectoral policies and in 1979–81 heavy industry output fell marginally whilst light industry roes by over 30%.[12] Overall, the effect of these alterations meant that the late 20th century saw high economic growth, with an average growth rate of approximately 10%[13] and rising living standards compared to the poor economic conditions under the Nationalists and during the Great Leap Forward. However, the rise in affluence reintroduced crime and corruption into China, such as the events in Heilongjiang where racketeering and embezzlement of public money took place, echoing pre-communist rule where corruption was an 'abiding feature of Chiang Kai-Shek's rule.'[14]

It would therefore seem that the Third Plenum created the most significant economic changes. May Fourth had no real impact on the economy and CCP policy prior to the Plenum changed in theory and application, but constituted largely the same outcome as before.

May Fourth changed society's values as people became disillusioned with traditional Confucian ideals and social structures. It also marked an 'attempt to redefine China's culture as a valid part of the modern world',[15] providing impetus for change. May Fourth ignited ☞

AO1 The student has here returned to the Third Plenum and is focusing on a sustained analysis of its economic impact and reaches the conclusion that, compared with the other turning points under consideration, this one resulted in the greatest economic change. The student is here demonstrating a clear understanding of this key issue and is supporting it by well-selected factual material, and is working at level 5.

The student here, and throughout this response, has effectively selected and combined material from a number of books, which is an excellent skill.

AO1 A useful summary of the importance of the Third Plenum in bringing about economic changes, when compared to the Third Plenum and the CCP.

the New Culture Movement. It sparked the creation of new iconoclastic periodicals and writers began using vernacular Chinese to make literature more accessible. Chen Duxiu wrote that 'Mr Science and Mr Democracy' could 'cure the dark maladies in Chinese politics…and thought',[16] suggesting how culture was transforming to engage in the politics of Chinese life, attracting millions of disenfranchised to new ideals. However, the Movement did not catch on everywhere and western cultural ideas were not actually adopted until much later. This emphasises the fact that tradition and conformity were still strongly ingrained in Chinese culture.

The establishment of the PRC substantially improved public health, expanded education as primary school attendance rose from 24m in 1949 to 64m in 1957[17] and abolished opium smoking, transforming society into a better place. The CCP's policies penetrated the family level, politicising and controlling Chinese society in an unprecedented way. For example, the creation of communes modified the structure of the traditional family unit. The new regime gave the peasantry greater social equality, destroying the former prestige of the gentry and the 1950 marriage law liberalised women, allowing them to divorce and to own property independently, which they weren't permitted to do before. Also, traditional culture had never been attacked in such a way before. For instance, in Shandong around 929 paintings, 2700 books, 1000 statues and monuments were destroyed.[18] Culture became propaganda, spreading the cult of Mao, the 'Little Red Book' the people's bible. The acclaimed 'Diary of Lei Feng' compared to 'Hai Rui Dismissed from Office'[19] exemplifies the censorship and manipulation of culture to follow Communist party doctrine, used to an extent previously unseen in China. However, the higher education system was barely altered, as under Mao educated personnel comprised about 1% of the population.[20] This illustrates continuity as it hinders the development of China as a modern global power. Furthermore, continuity underpinned the cultural revolution as it upheld conformity and the repressive nature of the ruling elite.

The withdrawal of state control in 1978 left the population more independent and the transformation into a market economy enforced new social ☞

AO1 The student is here returning to a consideration of the May Fourth Movement and is analysing the contribution it made as a turning point in Chinese society. The focus here is on an analysis of cultural change and continuity, in which, though undeveloped, the student's views are well supported.

AO1 The student is here focusing on changes made to public health, education and Chinese social life as a result of the establishment of the PRC. Relevant examples are given to support the points made. The student shows an implicit understanding that change happened at different rates in these different areas. Throughout, there is an appreciation that both change and continuity resulted from the implementation of the PRC's policies.

attitudes such as competition and individualism. It also made Chinese culture more pluralistic (with western influence) and with ideology subordinate to economic progress it had less tenure on culture as well, leading to a considerable outpouring of cultural expression, potentially greater than in 1919. By the 21st century this new culture had spread across China, reaching even the remotest villages. In contrast, whilst colossal improvements in employment and living standards were made in the SEZs, many of the peasantry still lived in feudal conditions as subsistent farmers. Also, although the 1979 one-child policy marked change from huge population growth during the Great Leap Forward, it exacerbated gender inequality with a rise in female infanticide and sterilisation. Furthermore, the communes' demise and establishment of a 'household responsibility system' reintroduced patriarchy. Overall, 1949 constituted the greatest social change, as did the Plenum, in terms of culture due to technology, which did not exist in 1919. The Plenum reinforced social issues that had existed since antiquity and, under Mao, the chaotic destruction of culture did not contribute to China's development into the nation it is today.

In conclusion, after considering their impact on politics, economics, society and culture it appears that the Third Plenum was the key turning point. The May Fourth Movement produced a significant change in ideology and Chinese attitudes towards existing structures and values. It ultimately set the foundations upon which future change was made possible and elements within both the establishment of the PRC and Deng Xiaoping's rule can be traced back to it. However, it is arguable that a change in ideology is of no significance unless implemented. It follows, therefore, that the greatest change was brought about with Deng's assumption of power. Politics and economics are of profound importance, yet the radical economic reforms (and, to some extent, modest political reforms) introduced, not only changed Chinese politics and economics, but had major effects on Chinese culture. Though the establishment of the PRC contributed to producing the social climate for China's development, it was the Third Plenum that made China what it is today. Deng's overhaul of the economy was the necessary ingredient in China's transformation into a global superpower in the 21st century. ☞

AO1 The student, in this paragraph, compares the impact of the withdrawal of state control in 1978 under the Third Plenum to the impact of the May Fourth Movement in 1919 with appropriate contextualisation. The whole paragraph is one of careful and well-considered analysis with a good focus on change and continuity. Judgements about the extent of change and continuity are supported by well-selected examples.

AO1 An excellent conclusion, reviewing the findings of the researched enquiry and weighing the significance of each potential key turning point before arriving at a balanced and supported judgement as to which really was 'key'. A good understanding and evaluation of argument is shown and chronological balance across the whole coursework programme is maintained.

Endnotes

1. Spence, Jonathan D., *The Search for Modern China*, 1999 (page 489)

2. Gray, Jack, *Rebellions and Revolutions*, 1990 (page 285)

3. Spence, Jonathan D., *The Search for Modern China*, 1999 (page 622)

4. Gittings, John, *The Changing Face of China from Mao to Market*, 2006 (page 176)

5. Internet resource: *China and the Four Modernizations, 1979–82*, a statement made by Hu Yaobang

6. Lynch, Michael, *The People's Republic of China 1949–76*, 2008 (page 34)

7. Fairbank, John King and Goldman, Merle, *China: a New History*, 2005 (page 353)

8. Gray, Jack, *Rebellions and Revolutions*, 1990 (page 150)

9. ibid (page 152)

10. Brown, Archie, *The Rise and Fall of Communism*, 2009 (page 440)

11. Spence, Jonathan D., *The Search for Modern China*, 1999 (page 625)

12. Gray, Jack, *Rebellions and Revolutions*, 1990 (page 385)

13. *Deng Xiaoping's Economic Reforms*, internet document

14. Mackerras, Colin, *China in Transformation 1900–1949*, 2008 (page 56)

15. Spence, Jonathan D., *The Search for Modern China*, 1999 (page 301)

16. Roberts J.A.G., *History of China*, 2006 (page 291)

17. Brown, Archie, *The Rise and Fall of Communism*, 2009 (page 314)

18. Lynch, Michael, *The People's Republic of China 1949–76*, 2008 (page 93)

19. ibid (p.75)

20. Fairbank, John King and Goldman, Merle, *China: a New History*, 2005 (page 353)

The student has used a wide range of secondary sources, all of which are directly relevant to the coursework programme being followed. They include books written by modern historians and so will contain up-to-date views and opinions. Where the internet has been used, the student has noted the sources they had found there and used.

AO1 The student has written a sustained analysis throughout, directly exploring the process of change in China 1900–2000 by focusing on an exploration of a series of turning points. An explicit, clear and detailed understanding of the key issues raised by the enquiry has been demonstrated. The student has read widely, including books and articles. They have used their reading to good effect, integrating the arguments there into their response, and using them with discrimination to support the judgements they are making.

QoWC The quality of written communication matches the quality of the historical understanding shown. The whole answer is clearly expressed, and, despite one or two grammatical mistakes, is an excellent example of essay writing.

Overall, this response is worthy of a **high level 5 for AO1 and would gain the full 25 marks**.

Part A

Level	Mark range	Assessment Objective 1 assessment criteria – level description
4	11–13	Students offer an analytical response which relates well to the focus of the question. The enquiry will focus confidently on the significance of an event, movement or individual, as appropriate. The response will show some understanding of the key issues contained in the enquiry, with some evaluation of argument. The analysis will be supported by well-selected factual material which will be mostly relevant to the focus of the enquiry. Selection of material may lack balance in places. The exposition will be controlled and deployment of the results of the enquiry logical. Some syntactical and/or spelling errors may be found but the writing will be coherent overall. The skills required to produce a convincing and cogent account of the results of an enquiry will be mostly in place. **High level 4: 13 marks** – the qualities of level 4 are securely displayed. **Mid-level 4: 12 marks** – the qualities of level 4 are displayed but material is less convincing in its range/depth **or** the quality of written communication does not conform. **Low level 4: 11 marks** – the qualities of level 4 are displayed but material is less convincing in its range/depth **and** the quality of written communication does not conform.
3	7–10	Students' answers will be broadly analytical and will show some understanding of the focus of the question. The enquiry will focus on the significance of an event, movement or individual, as appropriate. The response will demonstrate some understanding of key issues related to the enquiry but may include material which is either descriptive, and thus only implicitly relevant to the enquiry's focus, or which strays from that focus in places. The selection of material will not demonstrate balance throughout. The answer will show some degree of direction and control but these attributes will not normally be sustained throughout the answer. The student will demonstrate some of the skills needed to produce a convincing account of the results of an enquiry but there may be passages which show deficiencies in organisation. The answer is likely to include some syntactical and/or spelling errors. **High level 3: 10 marks** – the qualities of level 3 are securely displayed. **Mid-level 3: 8–9 marks** – the qualities of level 3 are displayed but material is less convincing in its range/depth **or** the quality of written communication does not conform. **Low level 3: 7 marks** – the qualities of level 3 are displayed but material is less convincing in its range/depth **and** the quality of written communication does not conform.

Level	Mark range	Assessment Objective 1 assessment criteria – level description
2	4–6	Students will produce statements, with some development in the form of material selected, which is relevant to an enquiry on the significance of an event, movement or individual, as appropriate. There will be some attempt to focus on significance but concentration on the analytical demands of the enquiry will be largely implicit. Students will attempt to make links between the statements and the material is unlikely to be developed very far.
		The writing will show elements of coherence but there are likely to be passages which lack clarity and/or proper organisation. The range of skills needed to produce a convincing account of the results of an enquiry is likely to be limited. Frequent syntactical and/or spelling errors are likely to be present.
		High level 2: 6 marks – the qualities of level 2 are securely displayed.
		Mid-level 2: 5 marks – the qualities of level 2 are displayed but material is less convincing in its range/depth **or** the quality of written communication does not conform.
		Low level 2: 4 marks – the qualities of level 2 are displayed but material is less convincing in its range/depth **and** the quality of written communication does not conform.
1	1–3	Students will produce a series of statements, some of which may be simplified. The selected material will only in part be relevant to an enquiry on the significance of an event, movement or individual, as appropriate. Selected material will be relevant only in places and there will be little or no attempt to focus the answer on the analytical demands of the enquiry. There will be few, if any, explicit links between the statements.
		The writing may have some coherence and it will be generally comprehensible, but passages will lack clarity and organisation. The skills needed to produce effective writing will not normally be present. Frequent syntactical and/or spelling errors are likely to be present.
		High level 1: 3 marks – the qualities of level 1 are securely displayed.
		Mid-level 1: 2 marks – the qualities of level 1 are displayed but material is less convincing in its range/depth **or** the quality of written communication does not conform.
		Low level 1: 1 mark – the qualities of level 1 are displayed but material is less convincing in its range/depth **and** the quality of written communication does not conform.
Assessing Quality of Written Communication (QoWC)		
		QoWC will have a bearing if it is inconsistent with the communication descriptor for the level in which the student's answer falls. If, for example, a student's history response displays mid-level 3 criteria but fits the level 2 QoWC descriptors, it will require a move down within the level.

☞ Continued on the next two pages

Level	Mark range	Assessment Objective 2 assessment criteria – level description
4	11–12	Students will thoroughly investigate the question, selecting a range of sources with discrimination and integrating their evidence into a structured and sustained argument.
		They will interrogate the evidence confidently and critically in order to identify issues and make and support judgements.
		Their interpretation and evaluation of evidence will take account of the nature of the sources and students will show understanding of the need to explore the implications of evidence in the light of its historical context and in the context of the values and assumptions of the society from which it is drawn.
		In the process of sustaining argument and reaching substantiated conclusions, the status of the evidence is carefully considered.
		High level 4: 12 marks – the qualities of level 4 are securely displayed.
		Low level 4: 11 marks – the qualities of level 4 are displayed but material is less convincing in its range/depth.
3	7–10	Students clearly establish the issues of the enquiry and select a range of sources to develop it.
		Students interpret the source material with confidence, relating it to its historical context. They show an understanding of the need to interpret sources in the context of the values of the society from which the evidence is drawn.
		In making judgements, students give weight to the evidence by the application of valid criteria in the context of the specific enquiry. They reach conclusions on the basis of sources cross-referenced and used in combination.
		High level 3: 9–10 marks – the qualities of level 3 are securely displayed.
		Low level 3: 7–8 marks – the qualities of level 3 are displayed but material is less convincing in its range/depth.
2	4–6	Students identify a sufficient range of source material to address the question. They interpret sources beyond their surface features.
		Students relate source material to its historical context in the process of making inferences and judgements.
		They address concepts such as reliability and utility with some consideration of attributes such as the sources' nature, origin or purpose.
		In developing statements in relation to the question, they combine the information from sources to illustrate points.
		High level 2: 6 marks – the qualities of level 2 are securely displayed.
		Low level 2: 4–5 marks – the qualities of level 2 are displayed but material is less convincing in its range/depth.

Level	Mark range	Assessment Objective 2 assessment criteria – level description
1	1–3	Students identify material relevant to the topic. They comprehend source material, drawing on a range which is limited but sufficient to provide a body of information relating to the topic under investigation. Source material is related to its historical context though this is not sustained throughout the answer. Students address concepts such as reliability and utility by making stereotypical judgements. In making statements related to the question, students use sources singly, paraphrasing the content to illustrate or comment. **High level 1: 3 marks** – the qualities of level 1 are securely displayed. **Low level 1: 1–2 marks** – the qualities of level 1 are displayed but material is less convincing in its range/depth.

Part B

Level	Mark range	Assessment Objective 1 assessment criteria – level description
5	21–25	Students offer a sustained analysis which directly explores the process of change over the period. They demonstrate explicit understanding of the key issues raised by the enquiry, evaluating arguments and – as appropriate – interpretations. The analysis will be supported by an appropriate range and depth of accurate and well-selected factual sources which ranges across the period, providing chronological balance. A wide range of appropriate sources has been identified in the pursuit of the enquiry and this material has been used with discrimination in the process of arriving at considered judgements. The answer will be cogent and lucid in exposition. Occasional syntactical and/or spelling errors maybe found but they will not impede coherent deployment of the material and argument. Overall, the answer will show mastery of essay writing. **High level 5: 25 marks** – the qualities of level 5 are securely displayed. **Mid-level 5: 23–24 marks** – the qualities of level 5 are displayed but material is less convincing in its range/depth **or** the quality of written communication does not conform. **Low level 5: 21–22 marks** – the qualities of level 5 are displayed but material is less convincing in its range/depth **and** the quality of written communication does not conform.

Continued on the next two pages

Level	Mark range	Assessment Objective 1 assessment criteria – level description
4	16–20	Students offer a clearly analytical response which shows a clear understanding of the process of change over time. They demonstrate understanding of the key issues raised by the enquiry and sustain their focus on those issues, with some evaluation of argument. The analysis will be supported by accurate factual material which ranges across the period, providing chronological balance. A range of sources has been identified and used with discrimination to sustain judgements, although selection of material may lack balance in places. **High level 4: 20 marks** – the qualities of level 4 are securely displayed. **Mid-level 4: 18–19 marks** – the qualities of level 4 are displayed but material is less convincing in its range/depth **or** the quality of written communication does not conform. **Low level 3: 16–17 marks** – the qualities of level 4 are displayed but material is less convincing in its range/depth **and** the quality of written communication does not conform.
3	11–15	Students' answers will be broadly analytical and show some understanding of the process of change over time. They may, however, include some material which is either descriptive, and thus only implicitly relevant to the enquiry focus, or which strays from that focus in places. Factual material will be accurate and relevant. There will be some attempt at chronological balance but the answer may not sufficiently range across the period, although some attempt at breadth will be made. There is clear evidence that a range of sources has been identified and information has been appropriately selected and deployed to support the points made. The answer will show some degree of direction and control but these attributes will not normally be sustained throughout the answer. The student will demonstrate some of the skills needed to produce a convincing essay but there may be passages which show deficiencies in organisation. The answer is likely to include some syntactical and/or spelling errors. **High level 3: 15 marks** – the qualities of level 3 are securely displayed. **Mid-level 3: 13–14 marks** – the qualities of level 3 are displayed but material is less convincing in its range/depth **or** the quality of written communication does not conform. **Low level 3: 11–12 marks** – the qualities of level 3 are displayed but material is less convincing in its range/depth **and** the quality of written communication does not conform.

Level	Mark range	Assessment Objective 1 assessment criteria – level description
2	6–10	Students will produce statements with some development implying an understanding of the process of change over time. There may be limited analysis but focus on the analytical demand of the enquiry will be largely implicit. Students will attempt to make links between the statements but the material will lack chronological balance and is unlikely to be developed very far.
		A range of material relevant to the enquiry has been identified. Information taken from sources shows limited attempts at selection and is mainly used illustratively.
		The writing will show elements of coherence but there are likely to be passages which lack clarity and/or properly organisation. The range of skills needed to produce a convincing essay is likely to be limited. Frequent syntactical and/or spelling errors are likely to be present.
		High level 2: 10 marks – the qualities of level 2 are securely displayed.
		Mid-level 2: 8–9 marks – the qualities of level 2 are displayed but material is less convincing in its range/depth **or** the quality of written communication does not conform.
		Low level 2: 6–7 marks – the qualities of level 2 are displayed but material is less convincing in its range/depth **and** the quality of written communication does not conform.
1	1–5	Students will produce a series of statements, some of which may be simplified and/or unconnected. The statements will be supported by limited factual material that has some accuracy and relevance, although not directed at the focus of the enquiry and lacking in chronological range or balance. The material will be mostly generalised and there will be few, if any, links between the simple statements.
		A limited range of material has been identified for use in the enquiry.
		The writing may have some coherence and it will be generally comprehensible and passages will lack clarity and organisation. The skills needed to produce effective writing will not normally be present. Frequent syntactical and/or spelling errors are likely to be present.
		High level 1: 4–5 marks – the qualities of level 1 are securely displayed.
		Mid-level 1: 2–3 marks – the qualities of level 1 are displayed but material is less convincing in its range/depth **or** the quality of written communication does not conform.
		Low level 1: 1 mark – the qualities of level 1 are displayed but material is less convincing in its range/depth **and** the quality of written communication does not conform.
Assessing Quality of Written Communication (QoWC)		
		QoWC will have a bearing if it is inconsistent with the communication descriptor for the level in which the student's answer falls. If, for example, a student's history response displays mid-level 3 criteria but fits the level 2 QoWC descriptors, it will require a move down within the level.

Index